"GO...TELL OTHERS ABOUT ME"

BY LAURIE A. DITTO

Xulon
PRESS

DEDICATION

Our God is so big. Only He can accomplish making something out of nothing. He can take a life that is broken and filled with pain and make it something beautiful. Then He can use the transformation to bring hope and healing to others. I know, He did it for me. I dedicate this new life (still with areas of brokenness and pain) to Jesus, because: *"We know that in everything God works for the good of those who love Him. They are the people He called, because that was His plan."*
Romans 8:28   New Century Version

ACKNOWLEDGMENTS

Boy Oh boy, that I could write a book. To me it is a miracle, an accomplishment that I know God carried me through. I want to thank the Lord, Jesus, for saving me, giving me a life, and then living it with me to make it extraordinary.

I want to thank my husband, Mike for believing that with God all things truly are possible and believing it enough for this book. I want to thank our children: Desiree, Krystal & Andrew, Phil & Amanda, Sam & Ashley, Carrie & Matt, Hannah & Jason, Edward & Marriann, Jana & Josh, Yena & Mike, Noel & JJ, Autumn, Nisha, Jenny, Michaela, Stephanie, Casey, Kacey, Annie, Alex, Vijay, Tim, Phil, Jon, Todd, Tim, Nick, Steve, Ben, William, Jane, Kimanzi, Maria, and Grace & David for letting me be a parenting part of your lives. To the next generation, Samson, Deborah, Isaac & Jerusalem, you all have stolen my heart.

I want to thank my mom for teaching me that 'pretty is as pretty does' and my dad for seeing a home-coming queen's beauty in what I believed was an ugly duckling. I want to thank my father-in-law for loving me enough that I am a real "Ditto". I want to thank my sister, Shanon, and my brother, Bill, for teaching me while growing up how to love some-body even while you are angry with them. I want to thank all my family. I praise God for each of you and enjoy sharing in your lives. May we all know Him as Lord!

I want to thank all my friends as each of you truly are a gift from God. I want to thank the parents of Makenzy, Samuel & Sarah for choosing me to be a Godparent, and to the little ones themselves for allowing me to play such a role. I want to thank every mom who has ever let me babysit; I now understand and appreciate the trust you gave with the responsibility.

I want to thank the people who helped me with this God sized task. Mike, Desiree, Julie, Julie, Marge, Barry and Jeff, thank you for your patience, love, and understanding.

I want to thank the Body Of Christ, especially Mike Bickle and the International House of Prayer for the safe place to seek out the Lord. And a special smile to Shaun for leading me into such an amazing discovery of the LORD JESUS.

May we all use the Love of God to: Go tell others about Him.

To all my 'favorites' I love you...more!

Laurie

FORWARD

Laurie's book reveals what we all desire deep down, to really experience God and His love for us. We are such an experience orientated people and often this is noted in a negative way. God, though, is an awesome, infinite, experience from Genesis to Eternity. He put the desire in us to dive into a journey of incredible wonder and unstoppable love. A journey that will never end.

Laurie's encounters with Jesus will show you why her greatest joy in the world is to tell others about Him. If you have never experienced Jesus or would like to dive in deeper than ever before, this book will push your heart into a passionate pursuit of The Way, The Truth, and the Life. You will find that you really do have a great destiny. I myself can't wait to see the next chapter that God will open up.

Mike Ditto
(Loving Husband and Passionate Pursuer of Jesus)

Chapter One

The Light of Jesus is Love

Jesus is like a diamond. The biggest, most perfect diamond there ever was or will ever be. I think that He must have a billion times a billion facets to Himself. Each facet is brilliant and could take an eternity to realize the significance of it.

I believe that each of us stand on one facet and get to relate to Him in a way that reveals that facet's truth to us. I think that as we spend our lives discovering the hugeness of even one aspect of God we can come to a place of reflection and begin to see those qualities on a much smaller and imperfect scale inside of each of us. I don't think that I am any more special than anyone else when I have my experiences with God; I believe that is the facet I have with Him. In fact, every time something extraordinary happens in my life I wonder why me? I know all my short comings and all my sin areas I struggle with. As I begin to explain, it might seem like I live one vision after another. I can only wish that I could spend that much time with Jesus. In fact the visions with Jesus seem few and far between. But I do experience God every day. I expect to. I can hear Him in a friend, or see Him in the wind. I go to church expecting God to talk to me. I live out this kind of facet, to look for God everyday, and to try to learn from each encounter.

I would never give away my facet, but I believe it is so big in itself that it can be shared with mankind and still have room to stand on. The Bible says "freely you have received, freely give."[1] I know there was no extraordinary reason why I was given this place by God, other than it pleased Him to do so. If I have anything to do with it, I freely give people the invitation to come and stand in this facet and be blessed by it in the way that God has for you. I ask this in the name of Jesus. Amen.

In April of 2000, Jesus delivered me and it was life changing inside me. Now as a qualifier I want to say that in reality each and every time Jesus has delivered me it has been life changing. But this time that I am talking about, I had been drawn by something much bigger than me to go to Kansas City. Deciding to go to something like this was unique for me. I made this decision while holding a postcard that explained a women's conference that was going to be held there. Just holding that card convinced me that I had to go to this women's conference and to the International House of Prayer (IHOP). I was so compelled by the invitation that I knew I had to do it! I had never really left my family before to go to an event, especially a religious one. But holding that card, I knew I had to go.

I was expecting the International House of Prayer (IHOP) to be something huge. In fact, at that time there was a building on the same street as the IHOP and as we drove by it, I was so impressed. It was maybe two city blocks long, and maybe even that wide. It had nice lawns, big lights, and lots of parking. The name of this impressive many story building was "House of.... Lloyd's". I thought this House of Lloyd's was the perfect place for the International House of Prayer. In my expectations I figured that the prayer house had to be this big or even bigger. Instead the correct address brought me to a small trailer.

The International House of Prayer was just a small trailer! I kind of had a bad attitude about the size of the place. I couldn't believe that God would hang out in a small trailer. What was so international about this place, I questioned myself? My initial expectations were a big let down.

When I went inside there was nothing real special there either. But the bathrooms were very clean, and as a picky bathroom person I was very thankful for this necessity room to be more than expected at this point. There was a small lounge area, and one bigger room. There were no really nice or fine decorations, no shiny mirrors, or golden things placed all around. In the larger room a band played up at the front, there was a large map of the world on the wall, and lots of countries' flags. This was the International part, I assumed, and my expectations were again disappointed.

There was a man standing up by the band who every so often would read scripture. He didn't look international and his voice sounded much the same as mine. It didn't sound much like praying to me and again my expectations were disappointed. It was loud, all the lights were on, and people seemed to each be doing their own thing. Nothing like the solitude I thought would be wrapped with God, and all my expectations of grandeur had me looking with a very critical eye.

There were some ladies dancing in the back. I thought that was really strange. I thought someone should go over and tell them to stop making a spectacle of themselves. Some danced the same dance; some danced alone and were acting as if they were the only ones in the room. Then there were the people waving flags. I had no idea what all that was about, but again, I felt embarrassed for these possibly mentally challenged people. Some people were sitting on the floor in what looked like a mental trance, others were doing their work at tables, and there were some normal looking people sitting in chairs that were in rows. Nothing like I thought the International House of Prayer should be!

Still, I had come a long way and there was a reason I wanted to be there, even if I didn't know what it was yet. I had to decide if I was going to give the place a chance or just leave and go to the building that the women's conference was going to be held in. I chose to go sit behind some of the normal acting people. There was a woman sitting closer to the back of the room. It looked like a safe place to sit while keeping my eyes on the strange things that were going on. Within minutes of choosing this spot, the woman I was sitting behind, stood up and lifted her hands up over her head. They were lifted as if she were reaching out to someone who wasn't there. Now I understood this. I have a friend, her name is Shaun and she is actually the woman who helped me find Jesus as my Savior. She likes to worship God this way. I had tried to lift my hands out in front of me while worshiping with Shaun, but I was consumed with what other people might think of me to try to stand with my arms raised over my head in public. I had asked Shaun if she felt strange when she did it, but she patiently explained that it enhanced her worship time. So the hand raising thing was not something that I was personally comfortable with at that time, but if it was good for Shaun, I figured it was somewhat normal for the worshiping lady in front of me.

Next, the woman in the row in front of me started waving her hands in a rhythmic motion. This was strange to me, but still more normal than the dancing ladies. Then she started talking in some language that was not English but sounded like gibberish. To me, she was interrupting the flow of music that was going on and really getting under my skin. I think she bothered me more than anyone else in the whole room because she had looked sort of normal and I had chosen to sit by her. Then she started groaning and making a deep noise that sounded like she might be in pain. Very, very, strange to me I thought, so I looked around for a new normal person to go sit by.

It was probably about then that I heard God in my ears ask me a question. "What do you want?"

Now I want to say that I heard God, and I did. There is always the question, was it the audible voice of God? I have to say, I don't know. What I do know is that I heard God, inside my ears. Now I suppose it could have been inside my thoughts, but I believe there is a difference between the two. Inside of your thoughts you get to think of an answer and even debate the answer to yourself. But if you hear a question with your ears, you are more tempted to answer it out loud without spinning it around in your mind a few times.

I blurted out my answer without even thinking; "I want to know if the words coming out of the lady's mouth in front of me are real. If so, I want it. If not, I want her to knock it off!"

Imagine my surprise and confusion when I started singing almost immediately a song in some other language that to my own ears sounded kind of gibberish. But in my quick judgment, it was cool! It wasn't like God took over my body. There came a deep understanding of the legitimacy of what I was doing somewhere deeper than my logic. I knew that I knew this was real and better than real, it was uplifting. I wanted to be singing what I was singing. The sound coming out was pretty, and it kind of tickled my throat and thoughts. I closed my eyes and enjoyed. I wasn't sure what was happening, but if it was happening to me, then it made it real to me. As soon as I could wonder what I was singing about, I started singing in English. The words were beautiful.

I was singing about the beauty of God, His majesty, and His strength.

"Wow" I thought. "God is so cool!" Then I looked around. There were still the strange people around me and I kind of did a quick look to check out if all of the strange people were still being strange. I had taken my eyes off them for a minute and needed to be sure they weren't any closer to me. I also wondered if maybe someone might be thinking that I was a acting strangely, but what was happening to me was real and I was ready to testify to its realness.

Then the questions started in my mind. Questions about who God is, and did I really have Him all figured out. Questions about the Holy Spirit and what a spirit realm is. Questions about God's ability to be everywhere all the time, or to know each heart better than we know ourselves. Big questions, that can and should take a lot of time to think on. Now maybe the questions were from God, maybe it was my own self asking, but these questions were in my thoughts. It's there inside my ability to except new things, that my mind began wrestling with the reality I was struggling with.

So the strange lady who looked normal in front of me might be for real. Even though I didn't want to believe it, I kind of had to. If I wanted her to believe me, I might have to believe at least part of what she was doing as authentic. Then the questions bombarded my reasoning. What if the ladies dancing were doing that because God was helping them? What if the flag people just couldn't stop because of the joy it brought? What if God liked the man reading scripture? What if the people sitting in trances were doing something with God? Maybe their stuff was like that song that had come out of my mouth. Now I want to make something clear. I was still in control of myself. I let God show me. It wasn't like I was being controlled, only invited to taste and see. And in being invited, I had said Yes! I had said yes to letting God show me something that made me look like a weirdo in my own eyes. I almost immediately felt a strong conviction never think, or call, a person a weirdo again ever.

Then I began to realize that God had asked me a question. Now let me tell you, I have wished many times that I had thought about my answer before blurting it out. I wished afterwards that I had asked Him for world peace or something big like that. Today I ponder, what if I had asked like Moses to see His glory? Still, there was an excitement and a great hesitation knowing that God had talked to me and that He had given me what I had asked for.

I left the IHOP to go get settled in at a motel and grab a quick bite to eat. I was happy but sad at the same time. I couldn't wait to come back. I was expecting great things from God. I was preparing a mental list of all the things I would ask Him for on the next visit. Maybe it worked that you get one thing per visit, or if they are in the same category you can have several. Maybe there was a cut off number like the three wishes of the genie in the bottle? There was a new anticipation in me and about this place that cried out for God. I thought again about the size of the building. Maybe God liked small places. After all, He had been born in a small place. Maybe He was uncomfortable in big fancy places. I thought about my husband, Mike. He is not comfortable when we go to a fancy restaurant and they give you three forks, two knives and two glasses. Maybe God was like this. I wanted to find out more about God. I realized I hardly knew Him.

When I came back the second time, just hours later, I saw new people who were still doing all the same kinds of strange things that I had seen other people do earlier, but they didn't upset me near as much as the first time I had come in. I looked a little closer at the same people who were still engaged in their time at the IHOP. They looked so much more normal than my first visit. It was just what they were doing that looked strange. Then I thought about some of the things I have seen in church. We do certain things inside of church that we don't do anywhere else. For example, we hug people. When I walk into the grocery store I don't hug the lady handing out the free sample of crackers with cheese spread on it(unless it happens to be a lady named Pat. I always hug Pat, wherever I see her). Yet, I do hug the lady handing me a bulletin inside of church. I don't say "Amen" after the teller at the bank explains how to fill in the deposit slip correctly the way I do when the preacher explains how to live my life correctly. I tried to grasp what these people who want to minister to God were doing, and thought that maybe this church's structure was just different, and these people didn't act this way out in the real world.

I sat more up towards the front this time. I figured it would be easier for God to find me there. I waited and waited and waited. And He didn't come and He didn't come. I started getting pretty angry with myself. "Man I wished I hadn't just asked God if the lady in front of me was doing the right thing", I grumbled. I wish I had been a little smarter with my response. I wish I had taken a little more time and thought about it. I wished I wasn't such a quick one for responses. Maybe God didn't like that I had thought the other people were 'weird'. Maybe I had better repent again. So I did.

And I waited some more and He didn't come. Then I started to really get angry. Maybe I was angry at God, but mostly I was angry at myself. How could I have left God? Didn't I think God was important enough for me to wait on Him?

"Can't you see I'm here waiting for you?" I thought. "Don't you know I'm here", I thought louder. "Should I move up more to the very front row?" I questioned.

I waited some more. And it seemed like He was never going to come, but what other option did I have? God was in this place and giving people what they wanted. If I left and went home I would be going with only the ability to sing in a new language. I recalled how many times I had heard about people asking God for stuff. The name it and claim it game. Now up until this time I wasn't sure if I believed it, but maybe those people were right. Want a new house? Ask God! Want a new car? Ask God! He had asked me I wanted and given me what I had asked for, but I still wasn't sure.

And while I waited, I thought about all kinds of things. Why was I there? What had caused me to come so far? What was I hoping for in my life? Who is God to me? What should I ask Him for next?

Then I started being afraid that maybe I had blown it. I had wasted my only chance to really talk with God. There was a sinking feeling inside. It was hard to wait, and it was next to impossible to wait without anticipation and hope. And somewhere in the mist of my thoughts, I was taken away. I don't know another way to explain it other than I was taken away.

I don't know if all of me went or if that place came to me. I don't know how I got to that place but I was away from the IHOP room and inside of an enchanted castle.

Now it was a beautiful castle, and I do not make an exaggeration when I say enchanted. The place was alive. It was more alive than I was. Everything was alive and there was absolutely no possible way for any kind of death in that place. It was beautiful. It was made of stones, very pretty stones, and very big stones. It was what you would think a castle would be made out of, but shinier.

I remember that when I was a girl, I would go to North Carolina where my uncle lives. There is a certain kind of a rock there that looks like it has diamonds and silver in it. I thought they were trea-sures. I always wanted to build my house out of that awesome rock. I had asked my uncle back then what it was and he called it the Carolina Slate. I don't know if that is really the name of the rock, but if you live in North Carolina you probably know what kind of rock I'm talking about. As a child I used to pick up many of these shiny rocks and bring them home because I believed I had something of great value in these shiny, shiny rocks. I always thought that I was going to fill up my bedroom with enough rocks to build my whole house, then the whole world with this special rock. I became a rock admirer after this, and have appreciated many God made treasures in the earth.

The rocks of the castle were made of something shiny like what I will call the Carolina Slate, but these rocks were bigger and shinier than anything my eyes have seen before. The colors in the stones were not just silver, but every color was reflected in the rocks. They were stunning to stare at and probably very valuable I thought.

As I took my eyes from the rocks forming the walls of the castle, I looked at an opening that was shaped like a very big archway. It was maybe three people tall and I don't know how I knew this, but it was proportioned perfectly. This was the entryway into a room that was my room. There was a walkway, or a kind of large hallway, outside of the doorway that I was standing looking at and down the walkway you could see into the room through the archway shaped windows that had been placed in the wall. There was nothing hidden in this castle. You could see into every room and I had a sense that there were no doors in the castle. It was a very welcoming place and you could go into all the rooms. I was welcome in this castle, so welcomed in fact, I felt more at home in this castle than I have ever felt in my own home. I was totally able to go anywhere in the castle and I had a unique relationship to the castle. Somehow who I am is a part of this castle home.

The room through the archway was a very large room maybe the size of a basketball court and this room was filled with beautiful presents. The presents were exquisite! They were every size, shape and color. Big ones, and little ones, and all beautifully wrapped with big bows and lots of ribbon. Every one was very special, and very shiny. As a child, I always loved to look at pretty packages, and as a woman I have learned to appreciate the fine paper and details of a wrapped present. I enjoy looking at presents, but I especially love to give presents, beautifully wrapped ones. I always like to know what is in the presents, even if it isn't mine. I carry the excitement of a child, but I try to curb that as a woman. I just love how a beautiful wrapped present can cause such excitement. I believe it causes such an anticipation in a heart, that something good is about to happen.

Standing inside of the archway of the room filled with beautiful presents was the man, Jesus. I knew it was Jesus, and even though I had never met Jesus, it was Jesus.

He was a man, and although I don't know the words to explain it, I think it was like He was a man made out of diamonds. There was light coming from inside of Him and it shot out of Him and it flew out of every pore. It wasn't like it had to wait to travel down His arm and exit out through His fingers. It just went out. He was brilliant, like a man made out of diamonds or one liquid diamond, or the sun was shinning on Lake Superior. He was more stunning in beauty than any of the exquisite presents or anything I have ever desired.

As He turned I caught a glimpse of the color of His hair, and of His forearm. I was surprised at how Jesus' skin and hair was so dark. I don't know why, but I had always thought that Jesus was somebody with light brown hair and bright blue eyes. But I think in this castle He looked how a Jewish King should look. Sometimes, as He would move, I could catch a glimpse of the color of His skin, but it quickly returned to the diamond brilliance. And this brilliant light exploded out of Him everywhere. The light traveled out away from Him, and nowhere was there any darkness. There was so much light around Him that it was hard to see Him the way that we can see each other. But He stood very powerfully in the archway and His light filled every room in the castle. I knew His light went out of the castle and somehow I knew it could not be stopped as it reached into the Heavens.

One of the things that surprised me when I looked at Him was where the nail marks were on His body. I had grown up believing that the nail marks that are on Jesus were in the palm of His hands. But the Man that I met had a terrible wound, healed now, but a terrible wound just above His wrists. That sure surprised me and I remember thinking that is not in the right place. Still, the beauty of Him was so captivating that my observation was not my main concern.

This was Jesus, and He was standing right in front of me wanting to talk to me.

I found myself trying to take in everything because this minute was so important. I did not remember being in the IHOP waiting to talk to God. I didn't remember anything about my life. Only this minute mattered. Being there I knew was the most important minute ever. Nothing before in my life mattered. Nothing of my life now mattered. Nothing else happening in the world mattered. And nothing in my future would ever matter but to look at Him. I was living for this minute to stand there and look at Him. I could have done it for my whole life.

Then I realized He was looking at me. It gives you a weird feeling to realize this. To be so exposed and to want to be transparent. To know that He is transparent and yet not have the capacity to grasp what it is that your eyes are seeing. To know He is looking and can see everything and that there is no way to hide anything. I knew He wanted to talk to me. I also knew that He could talk to everyone and every-thing. I just knew that Jesus knew every language ever spoken or that would be spoken. I knew that He could speak to all the birds and animals. I knew that He could speak to elements like wind and rain. I just knew that He could speak to anything. He wanted, and I say that again, wanted, to speak to me. Jesus said to me "Laurie". He knew me. There was a tone in His voice that was a tone of knowledge. He knew me and I wished I knew myself the way that He did.

When He said my name it sounded so beautiful. The effect the sound had on Him and on me was powerful. Like yelling the word "Fire" and at the same time whispering " Shh" to the baby you love that is almost asleep. It was like both of these but more. I have to tell you that when God says your name it is so beautiful, and breath stopping. It says in the book of Revelation that He has a new name for us[2.] I thought that if my name sounds this good I don't need a new name. The one He had spoken, mine, is perfect.

Until I had heard my name from Him, I had always been a little disappointed in my name. I didn't think my name was very elegant, pretty or strong. It just never sounded like very much to me. Not like the name Victoria. (Vic-tor- ree- ah). Doesn't Victoria sound very ladylike, important, impressive, special and gentle? I just never thought the name "Laurie" sounded like much of anything until He said it. Then I was so happy that "Laurie" is my name. My name was stuck inside of His glory; and just a side note, if you say the word "glory", you can hear my name "Laurie" in it. I had never noticed that before. It has a way of making you feel special. God likes us to feel special and He likes to place those special gift throughout our lives. It is wonderful how God shows you a special keepsake to make something that is a lie become a beautiful truth. The lie, my name is yucky. The truth, my name is awesome.

He said my name "Laurie". There is no sound I have ever heard as beautiful, as powerful, and as transforming as the voice of Jesus. Then He said "Laurie, give me that". It was so exciting to hear His voice, it was so uplifting, it was just wonderful, but…

I knew what He wanted, what He meant. He didn't have to go into a long explanation. When God speaks you know what He means even if no one else can understand. But you know. He wanted me to give Him the fact, the truth, the lie, that I was a smoker. I smoked over three packs of cigarettes a day. My head went down quickly. I couldn't look at Him any more. My heart did not want what His heart wanted for me.

There was no way, not even being there in that special place, that I was going to do that. I had tried to quit. For years I had tried and failed. And every new quit smoking product that came out, I bought. I never lasted. It became a subject of great shame for me. One time I had quit for a month. I had made it a whole 30 days and they were the worst 30 days of my whole life. I had dreams about cigarettes nightly and I was the crankiest person I had ever known. There was no way for me to stop. It never got better in those 30 days, in fact it got very much worse. Living became a question of "What For?" I mean I was all out miserable.

I finally gave up the hope that I would ever be a non-smoker. I think everyone around me had given up too. My husband, our daughters, my folks, my friends, just everybody believed that all I could hope for was to cut drastically down on the number of cigarettes that I smoked.

And there He was, Jesus, asking me to give Him that. Like it was so easy. Like giving Him my hand to shake or something.

I bowed my head. "NO!" and I started to cry. "NO, NO, NO!" Now it is easy to feel your worthlessness while standing in the presence of God. Especially when you stand in disobedience. It was a terrible shaming and lonely feeling to be standing there. I waited a long time. It felt like maybe a whole day. I figured that finally when I looked up that He would be gone. But He wasn't. He was still right in front of me. He was waiting for me. Light was going everywhere. It was moving all around us. And there was like a new brighter light filling the room of presents.

Jesus took a step towards me causing all surrounding things, including me, to shift. I don't know how to explain it but the atmosphere changed. Worlds collided. He moved closer to me. The only thing I can compare it to might be you standing out on the moon talking to me here in my living room. Then He took one step towards me and it was the distance between the moon and my house. That is how far He traveled in the one step, or that is how quickly He passed though worlds. Jesus moved and it took a second for everything to come into clear understanding. He stood there, much closer and so much more beautiful. He looked at me and I knew. I knew that I knew that He was smiling at me. I could not see His face because the light around us was almost blinding. His face was so filled up with light and there was no doubt that He was in love with me. I understood that the light of Jesus is love. Love is light.

This so much surprised me. I expected something so much worse. I expected Him to have left in disgust, or if He was still there, to be disappointed in me. I was expecting Him to say something like, "Well

then, you get what you deserve" , or even possibly ," I
knew you would let me down again". But He didn't.

Jesus said to me, "Laurie, all of those presents
in that room are for you. That is your room." And
His voice was even kinder than before, but now it
was hard to concentrate in the closeness of His love.
My heart was overjoyed and nothing else mattered
except the fact that He had not left me. My heart was
leaping all over the place because He loved me. Even
in my disobedience to Him, even in my mindset
against Him, He loved me. He didn't talk about my
sin. He didn't mention that He was Lord & Master.
He didn't try to put distance between us. He melted
me with encouraging and gently spoken words. He
spoke about my simple passion. It was as if He knew
how much I like presents and would speak to me on
a non-threatening level. I am positive there was no
underlying anger in Him. It was so beautiful to stand
in His love, acceptance, and patience.

He said, "Some presents are what I will give you
and some presents are what I have to take away." He
waited a minute for me to be able to process what He
was saying because it was harder to concentrate so
close to Him. "So will you give me that?" He asked
again in a gentle coaxing voice.

My head was shaking, my body was shaking,
and I felt a sensation to run, to run fast and far. My
legs weren't going anywhere and I was stuck to the
ground, but I was insistent on my answer of "NO!"
An overwhelming feeling of run, run, run, was within
me, while at the same time there was an unstoppable
force inside of me to not let go of this Love standing

in front of me, swirling around me, penetrating deep in parts of my heart I never knew I had.

He was totally at peace, a calm in my turmoil. So I waited. Just waiting for a minute in His love was a relief to the sensation. Breathing was helping, because I seemed to be breathing His life.

The urge to run stopped. Instead His beauty captivated me to try to see more of Him and just stand there. I have to say that after the run feeling stopped, I don't know if I was standing on my own. I knew that when I wanted to run I could feel the urge physically, but in the calm, I'm not sure that I was standing. Everything became effortless as soon as the running sensation stopped.

I started explaining to Jesus why I couldn't give Him what He was asking for. I tried looking down, but instead I think I stared at the light and it compelled me to empty out all of my heart and all of my fears. It was strange to feel shame and at the same time to want to share it with someone as if they could lessen it just by sharing it.

I could not stop smoking. I just had no more strength to do it.

I tried many times and failed every time, and there had been so many failures, so much shame.

No one was going to help me now; it was like the story of crying wolf.

I cannot fail anymore, or I just might quit in other areas of my life too.

I am getting older, and I keep gaining weight, and if I stop smoking I will get fatter.

If I get real fat, I don't think my husband will stay married to a fat woman.

I need it to calm me down.

I don't really like me any more.

I am not in control of my own life anymore.

I am very afraid.

And worst of all, what if you can't help me either?

And I gave Jesus reason after reason after reason why I could not quit. I didn't believe that even Him helping me could bring success, and I needed Him to understand the magnitude of my failure. I didn't want my shame to be around Him or associated with Him. So I kept repeating it. " I am the failure!" I didn't want Him to be any part of my shortcomings. I didn't want to link His name with my next attempt and next failure.

I kept staring at Him and His beauty of light. He was in front of me, but in me at the exact same time. His love is so completely encompassing. It cannot be stopped.

Jesus just stood there patiently waiting. He is so patient. His patience is so beautiful and so uplifting and every bit healing in itself. Jesus is such a great listener. And I am positive He kept smiling at me, even in what many have told me was direct and inten- tional disobedience. I know that sounds strange that He kept smiling at me because I never saw it. But in my life I have learned when the person you are with is happy towards you then you just know they are smiling at you. Jesus was very happy towards me. Jesus stayed. He listened. He caused an outpouring in my heart. He brought out reasons that I don't think I even realized I had. Nothing was hidden. He had the whole picture of helplessness and hopelessness. And probably for the first time, I could see the entirety of the helplessness and hopelessness residing and even controlling my life. He stood steadfast smiling at me. Never rushing, never a hint of impatience, never a hint of condemnation surrounded Him. There was only joy, only acceptance, only love. I say only and I mean that. Something was happening that I do not have a word for. One thing was going on and it was all encompassing joy, acceptance and love. It was non-threatening, but very powerful.

I have often thought about this particular "one thing" that Jesus uses. In the Bible He has a talk with a woman named Martha and He tells her how only one thing is important[3]. I believe that the love of Jesus is one thing and it includes all of the fruit of the Spirit. Often times I try to separate the nine elements of the fruit of the Spirit, and I can try, but when I let them reside as a whole I believe I am most Christ like.

When I had finished telling Him everything, I felt a great relief. Then, when that realization was mine to keep, He took another step closer to me. We can have a revelation of something but it can be just revelation. When we keep it, we become changed by it. It's like owning something. It's like children. We might know about children, but when we have our own, we really know about children. We might not ever be able to explain it, but we do know it.

Jesus moving closer this time wasn't the earth moving reality, 'bubble thing' that happened when He took the first step. But it was a huge step, and it carried with it a great distance and so much more light and love. His love was undoing me. It was so hard to concentrate; it was like ecstasy although I don't believe I have had another experience to even tell you why I choose the word ecstasy. The new level of light is beyond anything I have ever seen for sure. There was so much light, there was no possible way that even a shadow could have attempted to cast. I knew that He was so close to me that I could feel His breath on me or maybe His breath was in me. He was so close to me that the hairs on my neck were standing up or maybe He was stroking them with the electricity of His presence. Now usually that happens when something bad is around, but this time it happened and something wonderful was happening to me. This was good, very good. I never wanted to ever leave. Nothing in the whole earth will ever matter more than being close to Jesus. It is every reason to be alive.

Jesus said "Laurie, look inside of me".

I could see inside of Him now. And even though there was so much light it was like a movie was going on inside of Jesus' body. Now I don't know for sure if I had opened my eyes. I think it was as if I was already in Him and when He said look inside of me, I felt as if He was using something that really let me look inside myself. I could see life being lived inside of Him; the Him that is in me.

What I saw changed me forever. There I was dancing. At first I didn't recognize me. There was the most beautiful woman dancing with the man of light. The man was beautiful and strong and He was dancing with who I was positive was the love of His life. She was His reason, His reason for living, loving, moving. She was so important to Him she was His everything. Unless you looked at Him looking at her you couldn't see her beauty. But when you looked at her through Him you understood. He needed her.

This woman was His life and He would do what ever it would take to protect her life, even unto death. She was not going to be easily separated from Him, and His life and His very blood was set-aside for her.

Then I realized, the woman was me. Now I want to tell you, I have never looked so good as I did as when I was dancing inside of Jesus. I always wanted to look the way she looked. Nothing was really different between us except that I could see that He loved her. Inside of Jesus I am perfect, made that way by His perfection and love. I can not see that perfection in myself unless I look at me inside of Jesus.

I had on a tiara. It was so amazing; it shot light out of it, the same light that shot out of Jesus. It was a brilliant piece of jewelry, much like the ribbons on a beautiful package. This exquisite tiara crown had been given to me from Jesus. I also wore another gift from Him, a beautiful white ball gown. Cinderella has no idea the beauty of the glittery gown that God dresses His love in. It was made of the lightest material. It just twirled around me beautifully. This dress was perfectly fit to cover me. It had beautiful long sleeves that flowed down like something from a dream. The waist was an empire waist and the neck was very modest. It might at first appear to be simple but if you looked at it, it was the most elegant dress made for a queen. The material was as if it were a mirror reflecting its surroundings. Since Jesus was standing there it showed Him. It wasn't until I looked deeper that I realized that it was not a reflection at all, but Him in me, radiating out. I knew that as long as I wore that dress, terrible things like guilt or shame could never be on me. The dress was so amazing it was so glittery and acted much like a brilliant wrapping paper on an exquisite present.

I remember staring at the girl's ankles and calf's. The girl was bare footed and her feet were perfect. The same as mine, but hers were perfect. But how could that be? I never liked the way my feet looked but now through Gods eyes my feet were beautiful. But there, dancing inside of Jesus were my feet and they were elegant. My feet just as they are. They are not a mistake with Him. In fact He made them that way, and He loves them that way. I understood that if the feet on the girl dancing with Jesus were a different way, than they are right now, that would be the biggest mistake. I remember thinking, "Wow even my anklebones are beautiful". There I was, perfect. Long hair, tiara on, beautiful dress, gorgeous smile, happy and dancing with the one who loves me more than anyone else ever could. I understood that I was totally unique and rare. There was only one of me and could ever only be one of me. I was the precious cargo, and even without the tiara and dress, I was still priceless.

I am sure I watched Him dance with me for a long time. He never tired. He never once looked like He would rather be anywhere else. Just being with me, and me being with Him, was what life was supposed to be.

After I had studied her, and I took a long time studying her to be positive that this beautiful woman was really me, He spoke again.

"Laurie, this is who you are to me".

OH, OH, OH! I thought. If that is who I am to Him, then I have nothing to worry about. Nothing! Here I was trying to find something good about myself, just anything and here to Him I am wonderful, beautiful, lovely, and His! If that girl inside of Jesus is me than I have nothing to worry about with trusting Him. He even saw my imperfections and made them perfect. I was so excited. I was so accepting of myself, probably for the first time in my life, and it was beautifully perfect.

He asked again "Give me that". He sounded so sure of Himself. I knew He was so happy that I was so happy.

I knew that I knew that He was not leaving me until I gave it to Him. He loved me so much that if we had to start all over again, He would wait…He is so patient, so kind. He was so gentle. The thing that I had…smoking over three packs of cigarettes a day was a present that He had for me. It was one of the presents of what He can take away from your life. Things that I needed Him to take away.

Love, Joy, Peace, Patience, Kindness, Goodness, Gentleness, Faithfulness, and Self-control, are His gifts. He had them all and was sharing them with me. The second my thoughts went to "Yes!" We were hugging. Now I don't know if He hugged me first or if I hugged Him first. In the hug it didn't matter. I was wrapped. He wrapped Himself around me. It was powerful, peaceful, and beautiful. If you could live every moment of your life wrapped in the arms of Jesus. This is where we need to be. This is the place I long for either awake or asleep. He just held me, and He held me, and He held me. He was not in a hurry. He enjoyed holding me more I think than I enjoyed being held. And I didn't move. I never felt so at peace, so rested, so whole, so smart, and many other things I thought I needed. I never felt so beautiful. Jesus had carried this beauty from Heaven to give to me.

I don't know how long we held. Maybe I stood there a month; maybe I stood there a year. I don't know, but it was too short. Eventually I asked Him, "Is there anything I can do for you?" It was an awesome feeling, to be so full of love to be able to ask God if there was anything that I could do for Him. It was a question asked out of confidence. There was a knowing and a telling in me, that I was capable of doing something now. What ever His answer would be would be, I knew I could do it. He was in me, and would do, and help me do what I was made for. There was strength in me, a capacity to be. I was excited about the Love and ability that came from Him. I was so excited to go with Him.

He said "Go, Tell others about me."

This voice is life itself. It was not a command, it wasn't even a request, it was the same as saying to me "You are stunningly beautiful to me". It wasn't loud, it wasn't demanding, in fact it was so quiet when he spoke to me. It was an infilling. A peace and a purpose to move me in a direction that I was meant from creation to go in. It was right. It was good. It was all things fitting perfect in my life.

Next thing I knew I was back in the IHOP. Maybe only a minute had gone by. I don't know, maybe a whole lifetime had gone by. Maybe it was only a second I had been gone, but everything had changed. I was a new person. I needed time to understand what had happened.

I had been with God. It was God in a castle with me. Maybe that castle is in Heaven, maybe it's here on Earth. I had been with Him and He with me. He had met me, fixed me, and sent me out. As I said starting out, I don't know why it was me, I wasn't doing anything worthy, but He took me. He took me just as I am. He loved me just as I am. That changed me.

There is a place He can bring people to. I sure do remember the light. I remember Him and His presence and His presents.

This was as real to me, as real as every night making dinner. It was more real than that. I will live my life now for that man. And its alright that I am just like I am, Jesus loves me anyway.

End notes:

1- **Matthew 10:8,** *Heal the sick, raise the dead, cleanse those who have leprosy, drive out demons. Freely you have received, freely give.* New International Version

2- **Revelation 2:17,** *He who has an ear, let him hear what the Spirit says to the churches. To him who overcomes, I will give some of the hidden manna. I will also give him a white stone with a new name written on it, known only to him who receives it.* New International Version

3- **Luke 10:42,** *Only one thing is important. Mary has chosen the better thing, and it will never be taken away from her.* New Century Version

Chapter Two

A Gift from GOD!

I had a way to proceed and an excitement in me like a child getting a new bike and being told to go explore. As much as I wanted to stay in the IHOP, I wanted to go and tell people about the amazing man of Jesus. I wanted to live. I knew I was free. I had no idea what that meant, but it felt wonderful. And messing up didn't seem so scary now. There is nothing the man Jesus can't fix. He can do all things, I am positive of it. You cannot force His hand to run away, to quit, to abandon, or to forsake. He is so self-confidant, self-assured, and in control that He knows the outcome. He is so patient that He waits for us to know the outcome and nothing can cause Him to leave the path He is on.

As I walked out of the IHOP, I was new and renewed. My smoking days stopped. He took it away. Just like He said He could. I didn't ask for it, in fact, I thought I would ask for world peace. In a way that is what He gave me. He put my individual world at peace. To not smoke, this was strange. I had smoked during everything. I had even smoked while taking a shower. You can't smoke 3 ½ packs of cigarettes and not be doing something. My mouth felt very strange as a non-smoker. Right away I had too much spit inside my mouth. I was drooling while I was talking. I wasn't so thirsty now, and I was a lot hungrier. I could also taste things that I could not taste before. It was wonderful to be able to taste a little bit of salt on my food instead of loading it. In fact, I didn't care for salt on my food anymore, or pepper. Boy did food taste wonderful. I could smell things that I could not smell before. My nose felt like it did when I was pregnant. When I was pregnant with both of our daughters I was very sensitive to smells and it was like that again. Eventually I felt my skin change. I didn't need as much lotion and my complexion became clearer.

I'm new. I'm really new. I was so excited.

Delivered, what does that word mean? I had never really given it much thought. Not until it happened to me. Now delivered is a delight! I understood something very powerful had happened to me and for me. God had changed a set of circumstances and made a new path for me, a straight one. It was very powerful to know that I am loved so much. Delivered meant to be loved.

I also understood a little bit more about God. He is not a God to go to and get things from, although He loves to give things. He is a God to be with; a God who desires to be with us. He will take away things that stop us from being able to be with Him, and give to us things that help us to be with Him. I want to live to be with Him. But if I need things He will take care of it. If that thing is a new car, then yes, He will give it. Maybe that thing is a quiet time and He will give us that because a quiet time can bring us together. I knew I should not have believed in the name it and claim it thing. Inside I knew it was just a list of selfish desires. But it seemed the new thing that Christians were talking about, and if that is how it works, why not get everything you can get? This is not God, just the opposite.

The Lord said that following Him was not going to be easy.[4] But you know I judge my day on if it was a good day by how few problems I had that day. If it was a nice non-confrontational day then I tend to think it was God filled. I believe this is wrong. The way of the Lord is not an easy way filled with everything you want. Jesus had people around Him who really didn't like Him, He loved them anyway. Jesus had people around Him who were sick and needy, He loved them anyway. Jesus was such a busy man that He had to get up real early to have quiet time with God. Jesus was so busy that many times He did not eat. I like to think about what kind of life Jesus had. He didn't own a donkey, or in today's terms, a car to get around. He didn't own His own home, or an abundant amount of clothing. He didn't have stocks and bonds or a big savings account. He didn't have many of the things that I find security in. I like to study His life and try to get mine to look more and more like His.

I could have left Kansas City right after the first day. I could have gone home totally fulfilled with no regrets. I did stay and go to the women's conference, which also was very good. I learned a lot, some about me and some about who God sees me to be but it was the IHOP itself, that place of worship, that was and still is a life-changing place.

I left Kansas City wanting to do what Jesus asked of me, go tell others about Him. I wanted it to be easy though. I wasn't looking forward to the trip home. I had a flight from Kansas City to Minneapolis and then a 7-hour drive to my house. I kept thinking about how difficult it would be to live with my family now that I really knew Jesus, and they didn't.

Somehow I got talking to a lady in the airplane on the way to Minneapolis about the awesome thing that had happened with me and Jesus and the troubles I was anticipating with my family. I told her everything about the castle and how disappointing it was to go home. I explained how my family was a mess. The kids don't talk nice to each other. My husband is not interested in God. My life is dull there. And before I could go any farther, she said to me " it is obvious that you and your family do not pray together!" She said it so strongly I wondered if I knew her. Like a grandmother might talk to her granddaughter. She spoke with such knowledge and authority. "Obvious?" What is her deal I thought. I hadn't even begun to tell her my problems. She was steadfast to continue on. She stated that families need, no exceptions, to sit down and pray together. Each must pray for one another. She explained how words of life couldn't flow out when words of death are allowed. Then when we landed she had to go quickly which often happens in airports. I had told her about Jesus and the awesome experience, but somehow the things that she told me seemed just as important as what I had told her. I wondered if my family would pray together?

Then I had to go to the restroom. You know how airports are. The restrooms are not always close to where you would want them to be. The closest one was closed for cleaning, so I had to walk to the next one. Then something really stressing happened, I left my purse in the ladies restroom. Not on the counter or someplace like that, but inside the stall. There was a big round toilet paper holder and since there was no hook on the door and it's gross to leave your purse on the floor I hung it over the toilet paper holder. There was a line of ladies waiting to use the restroom and the sink area and towel dispenser area was busy, so when I walked out and left it behind, I didn't notice.

When I got down to the baggage claim area I real-ized I had forgotten my purse. I went running back to the rest room. When I looked inside the stall that I had left it in, it was gone. It is such a sinking feeling when something like this happens. My mind started whirling, and my heart started racing. It is never good to leave your purse, it is worse to think you won't get it back. So then I went over to the flight desk that was closest to that restroom and asked the people behind it if anyone had turned in my purse. I explained that I had left it about ten minutes ago. They looked at me and just kind of tilted their heads. You know the kind of tilt that says "Are you kidding me?" Then they said, "No, would you like to go and file a lost purse claim?"

Now I was desperate! You would have to know the whole story, but I always forget my purse. It used to be such a sore spot with my husband and me. It has always been that when we get ready to leave, Mike has to ask me if I have my purse. Many times I did not. It's not like you can hide it. You have to tell, so you can go back and get it. Many times we have had to turn around and go back, or ask someone to bring it or mail it to me. Now I don't carry many valuables, but it always is embarrassing to have to admit to being so irresponsible. This was just terrible. My keys to the car were inside plus all the other purse stuff. I was just sick. I couldn't believe I had done this again. I was so embarrassed talking to the lady at the flight desk.

Mike had told me right before I had left home "Now don't lose your purse!" and here it had happened, again. This was one of those shame things, great shame. I was traveling with a friend and before we had left I had given her a spare set of keys. I knew my tendencies. Even though they embarrass me, I did what I thought was a safety measure and gave an extra set of keys to my companion just in case. The 'in case' had happened. Getting home was not the problem, but dealing again with the weight of the shame, was almost crippling.

I was so upset and the lady at the airlines desk looked at me like I had lost my mind. I had to ask her again "Are you sure it is not here?" I was praying so hard that it be there. It was not. I felt sick to my stomach. The keys were important, but I had two credit cards, maybe fifty dollars and pictures of the kids. I just didn't know what to do. I could feel myself starting to cry, and the panic deep inside was beginning to win. I started walking toward the lost and found office to file the lost claim wondering how I could have done something so stupid. It had happened again, I had not paid attention and lost my purse. Just feeling the weight of my mistake was causing severe distress, and the beginning of a migraine headache. Tears streamed down my face.

What to do…who could help? I was spiraling quickly to despair.

All of a sudden there was this woman walking towards me. She was wearing a Northwest Airlines Uniform. The color was different from the other ones. Most of the Northwest people were in blue, but this one walking was in a red pants suit. She was smiling so big at me. I didn't see her at first in my state of panic and chaos, but she saw me. She said my name before we nearly collided.

"Laurie Ditto?" she asked.

Not that I noticed it then, but in recalling it, I sure thought that was a pretty name, even when a stranger says it. My name had become beautiful in this world.

Then as I focused on the person in front of me I nodded at her. Her smile was one of the kinds that light up a whole face. It was big and welcoming. I'm sure she could see that I was in a deep state of turmoil, and the tears.

She said, " I have something of yours" as she put both of her hands out in front of her. I was still trying to figure out why the smiling airlines woman was talking to me and then I noticed. There was my purse. She explained, as she handed it to me, that the woman who found it in the bathroom had brought it to the claim office and had asked her to give it to me. Then she said that the woman said to tell me that "JESUS LOVES YOU!"

I couldn't believe it! I could not believe it surely. The man that I had met in Kansas City, the man of light, of love, of patience, who had changed my life and had set me free, Him, He had helped me. I was sure of it. I was positive that my Jesus had fixed this situation for me. There He was! He had brought me back my purse. He had been with me in the bathroom, He knew. He was with me. It looked like a lady in a Northwest Uniform helped me, but I knew it was the Lord.

Removing shame. I wouldn't have to tell anyone, no one would ever have to know this really big screw up I had done. Then again, He was on my side, He was watching out for me. He was for me. So what if I messed up, so what if I messed up big. He is God, and God is bigger than my biggest mess up.

I looked inside my purse everything was there. He had done it. WOW! He really had done it. Some think it was the lady who found my purse, and some think it was the Northwest lady, but I knew it was really Him.

I was so excited, and I was again changed in a wonderful way! I was so excited I wanted to dance, to twirl, to love. I looked for the Northwest lady, but she wasn't there. Where had she gone? I still think that she just suddenly appeared and disappeared like an Angel of the Lord.

The ride home also had the finger prints of God all over it. I had a headache. It happens to me when my emotions soar negatively. And even though I had the headache, I could function. Being able to function with this kind of headache was in itself amazing. There was a peace inside me, different from just relief, but a peace that enabled me to endure and succeed. I knew that this was different for me. Usually when I overload, I have a melt down. I get a migraine headache, then I have to go to sleep to find relief and then I have to rest for about 8 hours to be able to re-connect. Not this time. I had the headache, but it wasn't stopping me. I drove the seven hours home believing God was helping me.

In my thoughts I was pondering how wonderful Jesus is. How I had needed to go to Kansas City in the first place but didn't know why. I just had to go. My spirit had received the call and I just had to go. I traveled one person, and returned another. All I wanted was to be by Him. To be held by Him. If He wanted to give me things, then I couldn't wait to get them. I prayed that I would be able to bring my desires in line with what He had for me. Still, nothing would be as important as being with Him. In just a few minutes, my whole spirit life had changed. In just a few days, my thoughts of myself had changed. Life was new. Something was happening, something big.

When I got home, I was different. Mike knew, Krystal knew, Desiree knew. But what was the change?

I told Mike all about it. I had met Jesus. I told him, "Jesus loves me!"

I know, that sounds real nice. That sounds like something you'll hear Sunday morning in the preschool class. But it was real, it was alive, it was really happening and I needed this. I was sure we all needed this.

I asked Mike for some changes in our life because we don't do what we need to. We don't pray like a family. I thought that getting Mike to do this would be almost impossible. But I was going to try. I explained that the woman said it was obvious that we don't pray together. He listened, and by what I know was the power of God, Mike agreed and said tomorrow we would start praying together like a family.

Mike knew that something different was going on. First of all, I was not smoking. That was a telling truth on the outside of me. Second, I was not stuck in shame over having lost my purse again. In fact, I wasn't worried at all. Jesus was the one who could and would look out for me. I knew that Jesus had everything taken care of. Third, I was turning my family into the direction of prayer. I was moving in a new assurance. Something was definitely going on!

So the very next morning we started praying like a family. I knew it was a gift from God. Although I didn't see the color of the wrapping paper, I knew that this was one of the many presents that were in that room waiting for the proper time to be opened. I knew that my family was being changed because of Jesus.

Today, I think that both the woman who said it was obvious, and the woman who brought me my purse, were each angels. Sent by God to bring me presents.

I say that God delivered me. I am positive that Jesus is my deliver. He did deliver me from cigarettes. It is gone. He delivered me from such deep shame about losing things. It is gone. He delivered me from the fear of asking for things that I feel might upset others. It is gone. He delivered my lifestyle into that of a prayerful lifestyle. He delivered me from much fear. Fear cripples, and when you are not fearful, a childlike adventure can take its place. All of this and the only thing I could do for Him will be to tell others about how awesome He is.

There is a power of God to deliver us, or save us from evil. Now I know the Lord's Prayer. In it it says save us from evil[5]. I had memorized this prayer as a young child, but until He stepped into my life and did it; I have to say I never really believed it. I thought it must be something that happens after you die, and He delivers you from Hell.

Deliverance is something that happens now, every single day. It is something I want, and we should all want. Deliverance is a gift. It should be seen as one. The beauty, and brilliance of a life lived in deliverance is stunning. It is a facet of Jesus and sparkles like the diamonds that I believe He is. Deliverance is of God, and it is love.

End notes

4- **Matthew 16:24** *Then Jesus said to his followers, "If people want to follow me, they must give up the things they want. They must be willing even to give up their lives to follow me."* New Century Version

5- **Matthew 6:9-13** *So when you pray, you should pray like this: "Our Father in heaven, may your name always be kept holy. May your kingdom come and what you want be done, here on earth as it is in heaven. Give us the food we need for each day. Forgive us for our sins, just as we have forgiven those who sinned against us. And do not cause us to be tempted, but save us from the evil one."* New Century Version

Chapter Three

Carrying the Greatness

So what does all this mean? Where do I take this from here? This trip to the IHOP and conference happened in April of 2000. And I didn't have the knowledge or life experience to really begin to process and validate what had happened. Now, I know that I know, that Jesus is real. No one can ever take that away from me. You see, an experience makes knowing something much different. It convinces you in a place that makes you an eyewitness. You know like in court when you want to validate something you ask for an eyewitness. I was an eyewitness to everything that happened in the IHOP and then in the castle. It doesn't matter to me if someone wants to express his or her doubts about the authenticity about what happened to me. That doesn't matter to me because I know it, and I knew it beyond any argument then. Jesus was Lord. Jesus is the Lord of my life and it wasn't going to change just because someone didn't believe me. I knew I had an eyewitness experience.

Even if someone had brought me an argument from the Bible back then, it wouldn't have changed my mind about God. I hadn't read the Bible, but I remember thinking that if this is the God of the Bible, I have to get to know Him. And if the Bible doesn't tell about this Jesus who met me then I can't believe the Bible is real. The Bible is very real, and tells about a God who loves us in ways we can't imagine. I can't wait to read and discover how much more wonderful He is. And this is true each time I read about Jesus.

There are religious people today who don't like what happened to me. They don't want God to pour out dreams and visions and for this kind of Word from God to be true. They don't want God to talk to you that way. But as I began to search out what this could mean, I discovered some amazing things that have impacted my life again and again. This experience has given me a foundation to say that not only was this real, but this is a powerful way that the Lord chooses to communicate with people. I believe the Lord uses this way to communicate with me often, to teach me something that I otherwise would struggle with. I think this way of experiencing God helps me convey who He is in situations that people can relate to.

He said to me, "Go and tell others about me." I have thought many times since being inside that castle that, "God they are not going to believe me." Many have not believed me. At first I didn't care, but knowing Jesus more changed that in my life. I do care. I want all people to know that Jesus is real and helps people and can deliver us all from terrible strongholds in our lives. I needed to Biblically back up my experience so that my testimony would cause even the most serious skeptic to search out the truth.

Starting out, just knowing Jesus is so much to grasp. I don't know who He is entirely, but there are some things that I know about Him. I try to tell those things.

Trying to figure out who we are, and how we relate to God is just as hard to grasp. But with the help of Jesus, He can show us much about ourselves that we did not know. Like I said, He is a man that in my simple terms is much like a diamond. He is brilliant and He is perfect. In His perfection He knows everything and He is so gentle. There are scripture verses that tell us that Jesus is perfect. Jesus is the perfect Lamb, slain for us.

1Peter 1:18-19, *"You know that in the past you were living in a worthless way, a way passed down from the people who lived before you. But you were saved from that useless life. You were bought, not with something that ruins like gold or silver, but with the precious blood of Christ, who was like a pure and perfect lamb."* New Century Version.

He is also the Alpha and the Omega.[6] He goes from the beginning to the end. He is that big. I remember thinking in the vision that He is so big, a billion times a billion times. Finding out that He is the Alpha & Omega all at the same time, in the same moment and you can't change Him. But He owns it all, time, space, emotion, life, it is all His to command, and He commands it according to His perfect will, from eternity past to eternity future. He is perfection. And all of it, earth, people, and destiny belongs to Him.

His name, Jesus, is so phenomenal. I always thought His name Jesus, was like my name, Laurie, a name to distinguish one from another. And when He said my name it was so powerful but to say His name Jesus, is like a diamond to our society. Our society uses it to advertise how much a man loves a woman. The bigger the diamond the stronger and more perfect the love. He is not interested in our measurement system because He is above it. The name of Jesus is perfect and whole, brilliant, stunning, holding and sending out all light. That is a powerful statement and that is Jesus. His name, His ability, His purpose, His wholeness is power. When we look at His name, we see that an Angel of the Lord came and told Joseph to name Him Jesus because He is the deliverer of sin.[7]

When we think of sin what do we think? We like to think of sin as being something that is far away from us. Something like killing. Not the killing that our armies do, but the killing that the bad guy armies do. We want those kinds of people and that kind of sin to be what sin is. In reality one bite from a piece of fruit was so devastating that it changed everything in the Garden of Eden. Literally, one seemingly insignificant sin changed life. It's true that Jesus delivers the killers, but Jesus delivers non-killers too. He delivers life. Now when I say Jesus delivers life, I used to believe this is at birth and it is correct to believe that. But Jesus delivers people from a life also, a life of death. The angel said to name Him Jesus because He is the One. There is no other deliverer. Only Him.

The Bible says that at the Name of Jesus, every knee shall bow, and every tongue confesses that He is Lord[8]. I always thought that this would happen in a time far far from now, on Judgment day, or when a person dies. This is not what I believe today. Today I believe that when you understand His name "Jesus", you can understand that He is a deliverer. It is who He is; it is what He came for. Jesus/Deliverer. He is the one that God designed the name for. It is who He is; no one else can do it. He came for it and is still coming for it. The Bible says that the only way to get to God the Father is through Jesus.[9] In our sin, we can't go to the Father, so that leaves us stranded. Until Jesus. There is no way around it, and when you need Him you need to call on Him and use His name. He said ask for it in my name[10], that name is the name Jesus. The deliverer of sins. Who He is the deliverer of your sins. The Bible says that when Jesus was going to help the paralyzed man He said, your sins are forgiven, pick up your mat and walk.[11] Isn't that cool. Your sins are forgiven! I never understood why Jesus would say that, and why all the religious people got so angry. But in understanding that His name is powerful to accomplish what it is called for, it is easier to understand that He could have just as easily said, "In my name, with the authority of my name, and by the power of divine capabilities associated with my name, I say Get up, pick up your mat and walk." I think that Jesus felt that it was important for the man that He healed and for the people who were listening and for us today to know that He is the deliverer.

Call on the name Jesus and you call out "Deliverer of my sin". I know that in my personal life when I understood that my sin was sending me to hell, I became very serious. I needed help, desperately to be saved from certain death, and certain hell. When I understood that Jesus would deliver me from evil, deliver me from hell, I bowed my knee, and I bowed my heart to Him and with my own lips, my own life, He became Lord. At the Name of Jesus every knee shall bow and every tongue confess that He is Lord. This happens now, not just on Judgment Day. For all I know Judgment Day will be too late. It is amazing how every person I know who has received Jesus as the deliverer of their sin, bows their knee, their heart, their ways and makes Him Lord. People who know Him as a Deliverer understand that He owns our lives. We bow to His ways even when we don't understand everything.

To be so brilliant, to be so perfect, to be without sin, that is who He is. To be so brilliant, to be so powerful, to be so loving, that is who He is. Each of us has a special place in the Heart of God. Each of us is so unique. I work with a pro-life pregnancy crisis center, and there is some information there that says that we are so unique, and that there are no two people ever created that are alike. God can make people the way He makes snow flakes, the way He makes stars in the sky and there are no two alike. We are divinely unique. Each of us is unique to His heart. Each of us has a defining fingerprint, or facet of the Creator, and He made each of us with a plan, and that plan is for greatness. I believe that if every single person who was ever made from Adam to me, and who will ever be made was somehow totaled and summed up we could still not grasp the wholeness of God. He tries to help line us up and show us who He is. He tries to help us see Jesus, a brilliant man, but more importantly Jesus is God. And each of us displays a piece of the heart of God. We could and should be amazed by Him.

I experience God because that is how He made me. People are very different and how He made me is different than any others. As I said, it doesn't make me special, although I am very special to God. The Bible says that He does not show favoritism to individual people,[12] and I believe it. He has plans for each of us, greatness for each of us.

Now I think it is important to take a moment and explain greatness. It is true that God has made us and has plans for us, but until we actually become children of God we are not in line for the greatness He has planned. What does it mean to be a "Child of God"? It means that Jesus has saved you from an eternity of hell. You are His and have an eternal future with Him.

Jeremiah 29:11-13, *"For I know the plans I have for you," declares the Lord, "plans to prosper you and not to harm you, plans to give you hope and a future. Then you will call upon me and come and pray to me, and I will listen to you. You will seek me and find*

me when you seek me with all your heart."
New International Version.

I want to make it clear, I am not one of those people who want to scare the daylights out of you and force you to choose Jesus right this minute in case of a terrible accident and you have to go to hell. It is true, it could happen, but instead I want you to choose Jesus because He loves you. Because He is taking your blame, your shame and your guilt. I want you to not just agree with who He is, but to allow Him in your life to *be* who He is.

I met an amazing man, Ray. He is a missionary and at that time he worked with The Voice of the Martyrs. He was in town and evangelizing on the university campus. He said at church that if anyone wanted to come and see what it was like to lead people to Christ to meet him over on campus the next day. I was interested, so I went to meet him.

It was the middle of winter and cold. I walked up to him and he asked me what I wanted. I explained that I wanted to tell people about Jesus. He handed me a big stack of tracks and said, "Give these to those people." Then he went into the building to warm up. I remember thinking that his training was poor.

Still I wanted to tell people about Jesus so I started talking to the students. I had my hand out and walked with them until they took the track. I think most of the college kids thought I was a little funny so they took it. For the ones that said "No, thank you", I walked farther with them.

"Are you positive you know everything that this flier has to say?" I questioned. "I can walk with you to where ever you are going to convince you that you should take a minute and read this" I stated. In my youth I had training as a pantomime and clown. I know how to walk and talk with people. So handing out tracks was not hard for me. I just used the skills I had learned before. In no time I had handed out the tracks that I had been given, I went back to the box and took out the rest of the tracks.

When I finished giving those away, I found the missionary who wanted to know if it was time to go. I said no, I wanted to tell people about Jesus and I had already given away all the tracks. He laughed and went to get me a cup of coffee. He was amazed that I had given away all the tracks already. He said that many people say that they want to tell others about Jesus, but when it is time to try, people find reasons why they can't. He was impressed that I stayed out in the cold, and that I had chased the kids down and got them to take the flier. He also explained that the tracks cost money and that if they had not really wanted one, I probably should not have forced them.

It still makes me laugh. I can just picture myself working the campus as if I was the Christian clown. It is funny, but it was good too. I can be a fool for Jesus.

Then we had a talk. He wanted to know why I call myself a Christian. I explained how Jesus had saved me from hell. That He took my place on the cross and paid for my sins. That He bought my life when I agreed to let Him take the blame. That now,

He owns me. I explained how all of His commands and ways are to bring me to the place where I could see that He wants me to be His friend and not His servant. I told how having Jesus as a friend showed me how in reality He wants to be closer than my best friend and be the lover of my soul. I sat in wonder as I shared the knowledge that Jesus wants me to be His Bride.

The missionary was happy that I was a Christian, and then he told me things that amazed me. He said that he believes in checking people. He checks to see if they really are Christians. He said that it is easy to tell the lost people in Muslim countries, but the hardest to convince that they need Jesus are the people in my country. He said that there are people who sit in church every Sunday and are very lost. He said that not all people who claim to be Christians are. That is why he checks on them. This was hard for me to believe, but I followed him for most of the day and several times I found this to be correct.

We went outside again and one of the first people to pass was a college student that I know. She was surprised to see me working with "him" as she stated. She did not like that he was on the campus and when he questioned her, she explained that she felt as if he were making the Christians look so confrontational. She thought that a much more careful, quiet, and respectful approach was the way to do it. He asked her " Do you believed that if you died today you will you go to heaven?" The question made her angry.

She explained that technically we are all on the same team, and that we all serve one God.

He asked her "do you believe that God sends people to hell for telling a lie?"

Now she was really mad. She was gritting her teeth when she told him that really bad people go to hell.

He asked her if Jesus had saved her from hell. She said that He didn't have to because she is a good person.

The missionary's approach softened immediately. He said something like "You need to listen to me, you are in great danger. Your eternity is not secure. If Jesus has not saved you from your sins, you are not a Child of God. Only Children of God can go to Heaven. Your unsaved life of sins will take you to hell. Do you have a few minutes that we can discuss eternity and Jesus and how His salvation works?"

She was so angry. She yelled at him that he was totally out of line and that is why she hates those evangelist kinds in the church. She stomped off. (A side note, I met with her after this. She would not talk about it, and insisted that someone as nice as me should not hang around with that kind of Christian.)

Wow, what a crash course in telling people about Jesus! I learned a lot that day. I know it is important to be sure that people outside and inside the Church have the true salvation. I check on most people now. It upsets some, makes many feel loved and on a few occasions has opened up conversation to explain Jesus. Not everyone I have told about Jesus has wanted Him, but when there is someone who does, boy oh boy does an unexplainable joy run through your whole body. Just thinking about the ones who say "YES" to Jesus and His ways makes me so very happy. It is important to be a Child of God first, then and only then can God line us up for the greatness He has planned for us. He created us for greatness, to be with us. The greatness that God has planned for us is to be the Bride of Christ. Greatness, that we would rule and reign with Jesus Christ. I think it is important that I clarify that right away and keep us in tune with the service desired by God.

I have not been a Christian for long in comparison to the years I have lived, but in becoming a Christian I have noticed a pattern that I think is very dangerous inside the church servants of the Lord. A pattern I am not so unfamiliar with myself. People are looking for titles. We need something to distinguish us, something that we can pin on ourselves because the title "Child of God" loses its luster and individuality among the body of Christ. We want to stand out and be unique in the greatness prepared for us. We desire a way for other people to receive our specialness.

I have been told things by people that I knew in my spirit were wrong but they would validate their word with their title. They would explain to me that they are a prophet, or an apostle. Now I do believe in the offices that God has ordained. I believe that God has called some to be Teachers, Preachers, Evangelists, Prophets, and Apostles. I believe it, because the Bible says it[13]. I believe that God places people in these offices. I have an opinion on how it happens.

I believe it works this way. God has called us all to be disciples, or students in training, of Jesus. In being a Child of God we enter into a family, or the

Body of Christ. Each and every one of us. There is no exception. If we call ourselves Children of God, if we call Jesus, Lord, we need also to be His disciple. As a disciple of Jesus we should follow His teachings so closely that eventually we could turn around and teach what He just taught us making us a teacher. We become a mirror image of Jesus. I am a disciple of Jesus, but far from being a mirror of Him. If I can teach you anything about Him, it is first because He taught me. We can be awesome teachers, a teacher of the Lord, if we can remain a disciple. If I remain a disciple by learning and sharing that teaching with others, it could come to the point where I will feel confidence inside of me about Him. When God's Word becomes the foundation in my life I will become a preacher. That I could preach the good news like Jesus asked me to do. When in reality I am still just a disciple trying hard to be a mirror image of Him.

When I have reached that level where I can preach the Word of God I can go deeper as a disciple. I am not talking about dynamically preaching. We know that people have God given abilities and some are better public speakers than others. I am talking about an ability, willingness, and desire to preach the Good News to people who otherwise might never know. To preach the word of God! To let God take over, use what He has taught me and do something that in myself I could not do. That I could stand up with the power of the knowledge of God and preach His way and His salvation, and accomplish what it was meant to. My heart should be the heart of obedience. Jesus told us to go, make disciples and preach the good news. It doesn't say unless you're uncomfortable.

As a disciple of the Lord I believe that God can give us a fire and an understanding about the lost world and how our friends and family will perish without Him. It is the Lord's Will that no one should perish! That Jesus as the teacher would put in us a love so deep for lost people that we would take them the Good News. That we could love them, teach them, and preach to them, as a disciple was taught. We would be evangelists to our families, our friends, our neighbors, our co-workers, and to the world. Maybe we would use words, but powerfully we would live example lives and again mirror the Lord.

As we are evangelizing, loving, preaching, teaching and sitting in the place of discipleship, I believe that God gives to men and women words of knowledge and words of prophecy to encourage one another. He gives them words of correction wrapped in His love and words of direction. And by the power of a word from the Lord these people become His disciples also and we grow into being the prophets of the Lord. God trusts prophets to deliver His words accurately. A prophet had better not mess around and change the Lords message. It is serious, the words of God. And an understanding that a prophet is still a disciple and that every word or thought that comes from them does not mean that it is coming from Jesus. This is important to note. Not only for the benefit of the ears of the followers, but also for the ears of the prophet.

After you have walked in that place with God and you know Him deeper; you will love Him deeper. I believe there is such a thing as an Apostle. It is a very humble position, to love the way that the Lord loves, to seek out the lost the way that the Lord seeks. It has been my privilege to spend time with an Apostle. I met a man from Mozambique, Africa. He was young. I think he was about twenty five years old. This man, Norberto, loves people. I mean really loves people- all people. He came and had dinner at our house. You could tell there was greatness about him. He would tell you that he is a "Child of God". Just that title pleased Norberto. He said, "He's my dad and I'm his little boy". Norberto loved people. My family spent an afternoon with him and watched him be loving and gracious to many. He was excited to be with people, all people. Norberto could teach us the things that God had already taught him, he preached to the people with conviction. He was an outstanding and accepting evangelist. He talked to all kinds of people whether they were wealthy or poor, sick or healthy. He didn't care, he loved them. He had prophetic words that when given started wheels turning inside of cloudy brains. It created a clear desire to know the thoughts of God towards us. People wanted to be by him and sat long after the meetings to just hear about his experiences with God. He enjoyed the people and desired to be with them. When he prayed people got healed. It wasn't necessarily because the person receiving the prayer believed so greatly, but defi-nitely because Norberto believed that God is good. Good all the time. Once when he prayed people would know the love of God and be able to believe in Him, there was a sign in the sky where the east and the west horizons both turned red. The people who saw it were so excited. He prayed many times and his prayers changed things. His prayers changed lives. I know because my life was one of the ones that he prayed for.

Norberto's life reminded me so many times of how Jesus taught. Jesus lived out what is called a five-fold ministry. Inside His own being He was a teacher, a preacher, an evangelist, a prophet, and an apostle. He is every one of these words, flawlessly. Jesus did all these things in perfection. He said we could do greater things.[14]

I saw Norberto love people in the fullness of God and in the fullness of the offices of God. Now I know Norberto is not perfect, and he is the first person to admit that. Still, what does the love of Jesus lived out in our lives on the earth look like?

I understood something about God that I had not before. His greatness in us looks differently than what the world expects. It was Jesus who washed His disciples feet. That is who Jesus is. He is the greatest power, yet the greatest servant ever. He was in each office in its entirety. Now I have seen people symbolically wash some one's feet and knowing God and His greatness I wonder if we really understand what it means to be the lowest servant. It's like when the toilet at work gets blocked. Do we fix it, or expect someone else to make it right. I believe Jesus would have been the last person eating in the church buffet line and the first person willing to help clean up. I think Jesus would have been the one holding an extra plate for the young mom who is trying to juggle three plates and two children. I think Jesus would have waited patiently while an older person wrote their check in the check out line and helped them get the cart to the car and the groceries inside. But it seems that sometimes we think that the titles mean that we get to advance in prestige in front of our onlookers. But that is not what I see in Jesus.

I think getting to be one of God's Apostles is like a step ladder climbing into the next office which looks higher but is really deeper and lower in one sense. Jesus showed an example about His greatness. He showed us to take care of others' needs first and if it cost you something then give it. Jesus taught us to suffer for someone else and that there is no greater love than to give your life for your friend. That's what the greatness is. As the Bride of Christ that is what we would be like, like Him. As the Bride of Christ we would love others and put their needs first. The Bride of Christ could walk out the nine aspects of the Holy Spirit. In the Bible they are called the Fruit of the Spirit[15] which means aspects that are shown inside a life. They are Love, Joy, Peace, Patience, Kindness, Goodness, Gentleness, Faithfulness and Self Control.

There are a lot of people running around calling themselves one of the names of the five offices. I believe that many of these people know that God has called them to greatness. I wonder if many people have called themselves names possibly prematurely. Not taking the time to be a disciple in an area, but jumping to the title and obtain a sense of greatness and distorting the true picture of the greatness of

Jesus. Maybe we know that we have been called to a certain office, but the actions behind it are uppity and haughty and don't really show a lost world the mirror image of God. That is what a disciple is, a mirror image of God. But I wonder sometimes what picture of God we leave with the lost world. Have we shown kindness unmeasured? Did we display gentleness to the hard and bitter ones whose lives have been in many ways tragic? Did we love everyone, even the unlovely? Did we pour out goodness to the wealthy and not judge them on their wealth? Or invite the homeless who is smelly and dirty to dine with us? Did we extend extreme patience and peace to the quick and nasty?

I could go on and on with ways that we, as followers of Jesus, have dropped the ball and that is not my intention. My point is that it is dangerous to desire and seek after titles and honor inside of being a Child of God and the Bride of Christ. Someone would never have to give their credentials if God were standing beside them. In fact Jesus didn't flash His but came down to our level to help us relate, become disciples, and achieve the greatness He intended from the beginning. So I want to make sure that I don't misrepresent that word greatness before I continue on. I understand that if God calls you to greatness He will help you. I also understand it will be a place of great humility. I believe in the place of humility, and I know I need to desire to get there.

End notes:

6- **Revelation 1:8,** *"I am the Alpha and the Omega," says the Lord God, "who is, and who was, and who is to come, the Almighty."* New International Version

7- **Matthew 1:21,** *She will give birth to a son, and you will name him Jesus, because he will save his people from their sins."* New Century Version

8- **Philippians 2:9-11,** *Therefore God exalted him to the highest place and gave him the name that is above every name, that at the name of Jesus every knee should bow, in heaven and on earth and under the earth, and every tongue confess that Jesus Christ is Lord, to the glory of God the Father.* New International Version

9- **John 14:6,** *Jesus answered, "I am the way, and the truth, and the life. The only way to the Father is through me.* New Century Version

10- **John 14:13-14,** *And if you ask for anything in my name, I will do it for you so that the Father's glory will be shown through the Son. If you ask me for anything in my name, I will do it.* New Century Version

11- **John 5:8,** *Then Jesus said, "Stand up. Pick up your mat and walk."* New Century Version

12- **Acts 10:34-35,** *Then Peter began to speak: "I now realize how true it is that God does not show favoritism but accepts men from every nation who fear him and do what is right.* New International Version

13- **Ephesians 4:11-13,** *It was He who gave some to be apostles, some to be prophets, some to be evangelists, and some to be pastors and teachers, to prepare God's people for works of service, so that the body of Christ may be built*

up until we all reach unity in the faith and in the knowledge of the Son of God and become mature, attaining to the
whole measure of the fullness of Christ. New International
Version

14- **John 14:12,** *I tell you the truth, whoever believes in me
will do the same things that I do. Those who believe will do
even greater things than these, because I am going to the
Father.* New Century Version

15- **Galatians 5:22-23,** *But the Spirit produces the fruit of
love, joy, peace, patience, kindness, goodness, faithfulness,
gentleness, self control. There is no law that says these
things are wrong.* New Century Version

Chapter Four

Is God Big?

When I think back about my first trip to Kansas City and the International House of Prayer, I know that there are times when we are drawn to something bigger than us. When I held the post card, in my spirit I knew I was going to go there and I was going to receive something I needed. Something God was calling me to. My destiny was waiting for me in Kansas City. A reminding of something God had placed in me before birth. A realization that God had set up for me an encounter to draw me into His plans for my life. It was a divine moment. Now I don't know how many times before God had tried to reach me, but I am positive it was too many to count. I wonder if it wasn't twenty-four times a day, once every hour. There are some memories that come vividly to my mind where friends and family, desperately and in a tender love, tried to reach out to me. They tried to draw me to the knowledge that there is a God who is radically trying to love me, but for what ever reasons, and I had many, I did not listen. Reasons like: Christian's don't have any fun. If God knew everything I've done He wouldn't want me. That is for radical people, and the list goes on and on.

The Bible says that God loves us at our worst, it was that while we were still sinners that Jesus died for us.[16] I think that as a Christian it is easy to quickly move past that truth. Yet, that's probably the most magnificent thing. In His brilliance, He can see us and He can see all the pain and yuck about us. At the same time while He is looking at us, He can see who He created us to be. He will deliver ways to align us back to who He made us to be.

I don't know why Jesus chose to meet me in Kansas City. I want to tell you that the International House of Prayer is one of the most powerful places I have ever been and I have been back there many times to date. It is a magnificent place and I would highly recommend that everyone who could go there. I have taken many people there physically, and told so many more about the place. Both of our daughters and Son-in-love have attended the school there, as well as friends children. Again, I highly recommend getting there.

Can I guarantee that you will have an experience like mine? No! It is silly to think that God is going to meet you exactly how He met me. He made you for your own greatness with Him. I promise you that if you hunger after God, He will feed you. I have heard it said many times that you don't have to go anywhere to meet God, that you can meet Him right where you are. I believe this. You know what, I really think that when you travel to meet God, He knows it. He knows when you set foot out of your door and you are after Him. Its like: I need to get to you God! I am hungry for you God! I want to find you God! Where are you God? And if the reports are that you're there God then I want to be there too. I'm coming for you God!

My life verse from the Bible is Matthew 7:7. Now if you need help with understanding the Bible, I can relate. I wanted a Bible, but there are so many, and I needed an easy one to understand as I wasn't sure how to read it. I was embarrassed for a long time to ask anybody to help me. After having met Jesus though, I didn't care if I looked dumb. I just had to know about Him so I asked for help. I want to encourage you to get a Bible. You can pick one up at a department store, but I prefer the local Christian Bookstore because they usually have many types to choose from.

Simply explaining, what you need to know is that there are two sections, an Old Testament and a New one. The Old Testament tells about mankind's fall from being with God and foretells about Jesus' coming, why we need Him and how we will know it's Him. The New Testament tells about Jesus. In some versions His words that were spoken from His own lips are in red letters. It tells what happened after He taught twelve men how much He loved them and helped them to become His disciples. Everything inside the whole Bible is true. If it seems like God, whether the Father, the Son, or the Holy Spirit, is being mean, you are misunderstanding the truth of the Bible, so get some help. I know this is over simplifying the Word of God, and I am sure that Jesus understands my heart on this issue. God wants to talk to us, and many, many times He does choose to talk through His Bible. I remember when I first read my life verse. Matthew 7:7 (find Matthew 7:7 in the New testament, The first book, seventh chapter, seventh line. Understanding your way around will get easier.) I was so happy! I thought, "Wow, I am sure special to God!"

Matthew 7:7-8, *"Ask, and God will give to you. Search, and you will find. Knock, and the door will open for you. Yes, everyone who asks will receive. Everyone who searches will find. And everyone who knocks will have the door opened.* New Century Version.

I remember thinking "how come no one ever told me that God said this?" I knew the first time I read it that it would be important and very significant all the days of my life. I need to do something. I need to ask and search and knock.

The Bible talks about people coming to see Jesus, that they traveled a long way to get to Him.[17] Now Jesus was on the move, moving sometimes many miles daily from place to place. People still came. That means they had to move around to get to Him. Sometimes they went to one place and He had probably already moved on, so many people had to move quickly to catch up to Him.

In our lives today I think it is easy to forget that people came to Jesus. It is easy to think that I don't have to go anywhere or do anything and sometimes this is true. But at the same time, don't you think it's a little prideful to know that we need God and say to Him, that He had better come to us. You better meet me here if you are really God, because you should be everywhere and I don't want to have to go around chasing after you.

I really didn't understand why I was going to Kansas City, I had never left my family before and we didn't have the money for me to go. And a lot of times that is how it is. We cannot afford financially to go, we can't give an answer to the why question and usually we have no basis for it. I have found that many times for me, this is what faith looks like. But my thoughts were, "I'm coming God, there is something special about this card, and I need you!" So financial reasons didn't stop me, but I think God honors our feeble attempts to get to Him. And He will meet us.

I have talked to different people and told them to go to the IHOP. Go be with God. I know each of us go after God with a set of expectations. It is really hard to go in need and not have a preconceived plan of what we want. I was going to meet God, so I wanted everything to be big. I didn't have knowledge of the ways Jesus meets people, and taking me away with Him was not anywhere in my understanding of God's capabilities. But I was expecting something big. I just believed that big was something that I already knew. I thought that big wouldn't 'Wow' me or change me.

I think I wanted God to be big, but manageable. I think this is exactly why I had such a hard time with excepting a relationship with Jesus. I wanted Him to be manageable.

My limited expectations left me expecting the International House of Prayer to be what I had allowed God to be. Because, if I could totally understand God, then I should be able to totally understand everything that says it is associated with God. The IHOP was letting God be God. They weren't trying to present God, rather just let God be real. Now I want God to be real. I want God to be big. If I should trust Him as God, He needs to be Big! For God to claim to be the Alpha & Omega, that's pretty big. To be the deliverer of the world, that's bigger yet. And even though I have an understanding that God has to be bigger than anything I know or could imagine, isn't it funny how easily offended I become when He won't fit into my expectations. Like saying: "This is what Big is to me, so you have to be this!"

I think He likes to show us our limits and His greatness. We are expecting God to do it a certain way. Then He makes sure we understand that He is not going to do it our way. For some people maybe He does do it their way. But for me, I think He likes to mess me up, and to use my wrongs to show me His rights. It is wrong to limit God to our expectations and deny that anything else from Him isn't really Him. So, when I went to the IHOP I know that I was drawn there. In my spirit I was drawn there and today I am still being drawn to the Lord. And if we are not drawn, then what are we being? Shouldn't we be asking ourselves some serious questions or asking those we love? Questions like: Does God have a plan for my life today? Do I expect Him to draw me deeper? Do I want His plan for my day?

Usually I judge my day if it was a good day based on how few problems I had. Yet the Bible says [18] to pick up your cross today and follow Jesus. We have made the cross something that is soft and silky to carry, something glitzy and decorative. Yet, It's very hard and rough and we do not always want to carry the cross that God has for us today. So He called me out of what was comfortable for me and sent me to Kansas City, where I didn't know anybody, with a bag of expectations that demanded that God perform for me. He sent me to a place that radically rattled my belief that if God is going to be big, than that big is larger than my belief. There were people in the IHOP that were worshiping God in many different ways, but because I didn't understand, I didn't want God to be pleased with it.

When my husband came back from a missionary trip to Kenya, Africa, he came with pictures of how people worship God. If I had been able to watch the Kenyans worship God with my own eyes, I might have thought they were loony. They give God everything they have in their worship, and to my restricted eyes I only saw an over zealous and undignified people. There is a true story about a King named David who worshiped God in an undignified way of dancing in a loincloth. His wife was not happy with that, and she then could not bear children. Knowing this true story, and that God does not like it when we make fun of others, especially when they worship Him, shows me it is not good to place my judgment on other people's worship. In fact, I think it is very dangerous.

Yet, I approach God with my set of qualifiers. And the Lord had to take them down and destroy my haughtiness about worship. People were worshiping God; dancing, sleeping, laughing, crying, speaking in tongues, moaning, pacing, rocking and flailing. People were worshiping God. I didn't want it to be that way. I wanted a controlled, quiet, serene atmosphere where God behaved according to a preset agenda. How often have I wanted God to be normal, something I can fit into my ability to know all things? If He won't fit into what I think is normal, what I think is decent, and what I think is honorable, and if He tries to step outside of my parameters, then, I won't believe Him. I won't believe, I think its weird, and wrong, and of course God would want me comfortable at all times- right?

I remember one time while serving on a school board an issue came up where we were looking at renaming an elementary school after a local person. He was a Christian and an upstanding pillar of the community. The board president had asked that we come together and present a unanimous vote, and if we were not in unison to let him know ahead of time. I contacted the president to let him know that although I respected the man who's name we were considering, I felt strongly that giving the school his name would be wrong. My understanding of the Bible was that God said to let our good deeds shine out before all men so that they might see, then give all glory and honor to your father in heaven.[19] At the board meeting the president asked for a unanimous vote knowing what I had already told him. I explained to the whole board that I was not in agreement with the unanimous vote and felt that instead we should use the majority vote. I then tried explaining why I felt it would disrespect the man and our God. This caused some disagreement, and at the meeting the unanimous vote was called.

The man was a good man they said. We should be so lucky to have more men like him in our community. God would be well pleased that one of His servants was such an influence in the community. I agreed with these statements. Still, I insisted that by my understanding, who should receive the glory from the man's life is God.

There was a fellow board member who was so upset with me that in her opinion I had poor judgment. And she offered that we re-vote to help me come up with what was the correct thing to do. It was for me one of the hardest and lonely times. I could not explain clearly, and I was definitely out numbered. In the final vote, I voted against naming the school after my Christian brother. The vote was six to one. The motion was carried. This one board member became even more upset at me. The statement that she made to me rings inside my ears so many times. I understand her statement. I use to believe like she believes. She said: " If that is who God is, then I don't want anything to do with Him!"

It was a hard moment. I shook inside with conflicting interests. I wanted to be liked by the people in the room that I could see and the God that I could not see. I nodded at her. There was nothing else for me to do or say. I had prayed that God would answer her through me, but He was silent. I knew I could try to speak for Him and like usual when I try to speak for God I fail.

You see we don't want a big God. We want God to be who we have made Him to be, to be someone that we can explain. If He is anything we don't like then we take the stand that I'm done God. I'm done with you and your ways.

I went home feeling sick. I prayed hard that God would give me an answer to the statement. I needed to know. I myself had thought that same thing how many times before. The idea that it will be my way or the highway. And more than likely this would not be the last time I would ever hear this statement. From others or in my own ways of limiting God. It wasn't until I prayed fervently for the person's salvation that I believe God gave me the answer to the statement.

See God doesn't care if we look good. I wanted an answer from God to show the other board member, but the Lord knew my heart. He knew I wouldn't have corrected her in love, as I didn't love her. I just wanted to put her in her place. I wanted to be right. I wanted to use God's bigness and different ways of doing things to make myself look good. But God wanted me to love the people, to love her. Then I started to understand that God's bigness is not for me to use to argue with someone. God is radically in love with all the people on the board, and He is longing to be in a right relationship with them. When I understood this, He shared the answer with me.

"If that is who God is, then I don't want anything to do with Him!" is the statement.

"It is who God is, and His ways are not your ways, and I pray, that you get to know Him so that you might never be apart from Him" is the answer.

God is Big! His ways are not our ways, and many times what He is doing is changing us, not the people we think He should. Many times His bigness can be seen through us if we don't limit Him.

End notes:

16- **Romans 5:8,** *but God demonstrates his own love for us in this: While we were still sinners, Christ died for us.* New International Version

17- **John 4:47 & 51-53.** *vs 47,When this man heard that Jesus had arrived in Galilee from Judea, he went to him and begged him to come and heal his son, who was close to death. vs.51-53, While he was still on the way, his servant met him with the news that his boy was living. When he inquired as to the time when his son got better, they said to him, "The fever left him yesterday at the seventh hour." Then the father realized that this was the exact time at which Jesus had said, "Your son will live."* New International Version

18- **Mark 8:34,** *Then he called the crowd to him along with his disciples and said: "If anyone would come after me, he must deny himself and take up his cross and follow me.* New International Version

19- **Matthew 5:16,** *In the same way, you should be a light for other people. Live so that they will see the good things you do and will praise your Father in heaven.* New Century Version.

Chapter Five

A Gift

I pray that I will never forget the vision that I had with Jesus in the castle, mainly because He told me to tell others. But also because it is such a beautiful castle and it brings such joy to me to know that He has prepared a place for me. The Bible says that Jesus went to prepare a place for us in His Fathers home.[20] Wow! That we would have a room inside of God's house. When I read it in the Bible I was so happy. For two reasons. One, it is going to happen. Jesus said it, and He always means what He says and says what He means. He said that heaven and earth shall pass away but His words would last forever. Pretty powerful words. So, it will happen!

The second reason I was so happy was that the Bible backed up my experience. Not that the Bible relived my experience, but it says that He has a room waiting for me and in my vision He took me there. Right now my room is filled with exceptional presents that are for my time here on earth. But like most presents, you don't know what's in them until you open them.

You know I have thought many times about the question that God asked me, "What do you want?" And I've wished many times that I had answered differently. Now, I know that God wasn't asking me because He needed to know. He never asks a question looking for the answer. He already knows everything. Was He asking me the question because He wanted me to know the answer? Did God want me to know that the gift of tongues is real? To know that all the so called "crazies", who will speak in gibberish that I don't understand, is the real deal?

Yes! He did want me to know that this gift of His is the real deal and He wants us all to know that the things of His are true. But I don't think that's why He asked me the question. I am sure He knew what would happen. The Bible tells us this too, that God knows everything that is going to happen.

I think God knew that I needed to know that He truly is a powerful God and that there are things about Him that I don't know. I think He wanted me to put Him in a rightful place of awe. That place is to be in awe of God, to study Him through eyes of wonder and view Him as capable of all things. Let me clarify. It wasn't the things about Him that He was after. He wanted me to know Him. He wanted a relationship with me, a relationship where I wanted to know Him, and a relationship where I would love and respect Him. You know if you think about it, how many relationships do we value in our life. It's the ones that we respect. In fact the people we talk to the most and want to be around the most are the ones that we respect and love. What causes us to respect someone? It's the things we know about them, but if we don't know them we often times don't respect them. Once we know someone it is easier to fall in love with them. God wanted a love relationship with me. He knew that I would come. He knows me so well. He knew what would cause me to come, so He allowed it to happen.

God's gift of Tongues is something that upsets some people. I remember that when I found out God had gifts, I wanted them all. My husband wanted most, but not the gift of tongues. I was surprised. I told him so. See, I figure that if God has a gift, it has got to be wonderful and what fools we would be to not want something just because we don't understand it all. I told him that I think he was being very prideful to insult God and insinuate that His gifts are bad, or worthless. He agreed, and through prayer, God granted him the gift of tongues and he now treasures it.

I am sad to say that I came and sat there in the IHOP waiting for Him to fill my list of wants. As if He is some kind of sugar daddy. But He knew that I would come for things that I wanted. It is where I was and I think that many people come to a real knowledge of God this way. I don't think it hurts His feelings that we try to use Him. Because He knows that at times we don't know any better. It is totally up to God if He is going to let us use Him or not.

It's like hearing Jesus say, "Father forgive them, they don't know what they are doing."

I acted ridiculously and selfishly to go sit with my lists of demands. His desire was still for me to know Him. God will not be manipulated. I say this just to make it clear there is no condemnation from God on this issue. He used my weakness to draw me closer to Him. It worked and it has always worked on me. I wish I could say that this doesn't still happen to me, but it does. I go hard after God when I want something. Whether I get it or not is totally up to Him.

Something else I didn't know about God is that He can take you somewhere. He can take you to places in reality, in dreams, and in visions. It still causes my reality to jump into over load when I realize that He can do something so supernatural. There is no other way to get to the place that Jesus was in unless He calls you there. That Jesus can cross all boundaries and can pass you through all boundaries is amazing. To know that He is not limited by time, space, and gravity is so mind-boggling. I know that He is not limited by anything. He is God.

The Bible says that when Jesus left His Apostles, that He was going to prepare a place for them. When I read this it gave me understanding that He could and if He said it then He would. I got to see a place prepared for me, filled with presents. The thought that He has them for me is an amazing thought in itself. It is so uplifting to know that He wants to give presents to people. It makes me happy to think this. I like to give presents to people. In this way, I am like Jesus, I am like God the Father, and I am like the Holy Spirit. The only way to be like someone is to learn to be like him. Maybe this is one of the things that God knit inside of each of us when He was forming us inside of our mother's womb.

Every day that God gives us is a present. Each day is something new, a way to start over. A new present is waiting for us. It is a sunrise away. To know it is as easy to start over. A repentant heart is truly amazing.

But like every present it is only useful if you open it. I enjoy looking at presents and the anticipation for a gift can be wonderful, but eventually we need to open the presents. The present is useless unless we open it.

Sometimes we get stuck, wanting someone else's present and not being very interested in the present that is for us. I remember a time when our girls were small and I watched this play out. It was Christmas time and I had switched the name-tags on each of their presents. My thought was that if they were being snoopy that they wouldn't really figure anything out because they would be snooping with the wrong gifts.

You know there is a joy as a parent to watch your child open good gifts that you have saved and denied yourself for. You really don't want to miss their excitement as they open the gift. I think God is like this you know. I think God orchestrates times and events just to give us a present. He is mighty enough to do it, and delights in His gifts enough to make it happen.

It was Christmas Eve and every Christmas Eve my girls would get to open up two presents. They were usually very beautifully wrapped. Inside one was always a new pair of pajamas. The reason why they always got new pajamas was so that on Christmas morning they would not look like little street urchins in old tattered and torn clothes when we were taking their picture. The other present was their one big thing. The girls learned young that one present was going to be pajamas, so they were really only excited over one present even though I tried hard to search out just the right pair of pajamas. Today, they so enjoy the pajamas and especially when they know that Dad picked them out.

So all the days up until this particular Christmas our oldest daughter, Krystal, sat and held the presents that were in reality her sister Desiree's. When it finally came to be Christmas Eve night they ran to get their presents and then I broke it to them that they needed to switch gifts. I explained what I had done and tried to help them release the gifts they were holding.

They did not understand my reasoning, but the littlest one gave her presents quickly and put her arms out for the ones that were hers. Our oldest daughter on the other hand was so upset. She did not want the presents that she had believed were her sisters.

When our youngest daughter, Desiree, opened her small gift, she was so delighted to find her pajamas. Desiree was several sizes smaller than Krystal then and her idea of special was characters that Krystal would have thought was babyish. Still Krystal cried because Desiree had opened a present that Krystal believed was hers. Krystal refused to open her own and although we explained the fact that the pajamas were Desiree's favorite color and size and coaxed Krystal to open the gift that was sure to please her. She refused.

92

At first we thought it was kind of funny. Then we gave Desiree permission to open her second present. Krystal howled with the injustice of it. Now of the four presents there, this present was the biggest one and under the wrapping paper was a box with the picture of the vinyl playhouse that was inside. It was a piece of vinyl that you put over a plastic frame that took some time to figure out. It had a door cut out and some windows. Desiree could easily sit inside and hold a tea party or play grocery store and there was enough room for her sister as well. It was just what Desiree wanted. In fact Krystal had received one a few years earlier and played it to pieces, literally.

Krystal was so upset. She had huge crocodile tears streaming down her face. She sat holding the box that Desiree's playhouse had come in and kept crying. When we tried talking to her all she could say was that we gave Desiree her present.

It wasn't funny anymore. We tried and tried to get her to open her own presents, first gently, then with much more coaxing.

She could not get past the fact that someone else had opened her present and was going to keep it. It was in her beliefs. Now all she felt was deep injustice and pain.

We tried until there was no patience left in us and probably no tears left in her. It was so unsettling. Krystal was so angry, so put out, so jealous of her sister. She had crossed over into a place where reason was not working. There was nothing to do but let her finish her fit. We put her in her room hoping it could help her to calm down so she could open her presents.

We had gotten Krystal her own compound bow and arrows. We hunted all over for it. It was just her size and everything worked just like Dad's. She was a Daddy's girl and would love being able to shoot like him. Mike had set up a shooting range downstairs in the basement so that she could immediately go down and shoot with Dad. She loved to pretend hunt with Dad. Many times she sighted the squirrels and chipmunks while the two of them went on walks, or hunting as Krystal called it. Mike often told her what a good eye she had. She insisted that she also had a good aim. Mike was just as excited to give her the gift of the compound bow, as we knew she would be to get it. Maybe Mike was even more excited about her getting this gift. It would enable them to spend more time together. Him helping her get good at what she wanted to be good at is what Mike was waiting for. He had planned on spending a few hours downstairs Christmas Eve. I knew it would only be probably thirty minutes. The girls never lasted as long as Dad could.

Eventually it was bedtime. What a contrast between our two girls. Desiree was so happy. She had played with and ate inside her house. Mom and Dad had both played inside her house. She was so delighted. She opened her gift and said what became our joy to remember every time a present is given. Desiree would open a present and say, " Oh, it's just what I always wanted………what is it?"

Krystal on the other hand was miserable. She stayed in her room. She refused to play with Desiree and was missing out on a wonderful time. She had even missed nighttime snack because she was stuck in her thinking.

Krystal did not want to go to bed and really we didn't want her to go to sleep so upset. Because it was bedtime she relented and said that she would open the new pair of pj's that she already knew were inside the small package. Mike and I did not enjoy watching her open the gift. We were already so spent from all her crying that it was not so joyous even though they were her favorite color and the "grown up kind" that she had seen in the magazine.

Between her body sobbing we helped her put on the silky, princess pajamas. Next she decided she would open her gift. We waited knowing that now there was no time for her to try it out and even if it wasn't so late, Mike said that in her state of mind he was not going to try to instruct her. Safety needs a clear mind.

Krystal couldn't believe her eyes. It was something she couldn't have even thought of. She had no idea they made things like this for children. It was better than her best wishes. The tears stopped, but her body convulsing couldn't. She was so happy to see the gift and so pooped out she couldn't use it.

"When can I use it Daddy?" she asked Mike.

We took her down stairs and showed her the range and explained that tomorrow she could try.

That night she said she was sorry. She had thought that we only loved Desiree, and had good things for only her. She was so upset because she didn't believe anymore that she is our favorite. Our girls use to have disagreements as to which one was our favorite. Each believed she was. It was a powerful place of self confidence to each child but when Krystal stopped believing it, she opened a door to deep despair. It was amazing that a child could explain so clearly what we adults have a hard time realizing.

It is quite a story to tell now, but we can learn a lot from Krystal. Many times this is exactly how we treat God. We want someone else's present. We desire someone else's present so much that we become jealous and hateful toward the other person. We are positive that God intended that gift to be for us so we fight and try to get it. God is not going to give it to us no matter how big of a stink we throw. And we miss out on the joy, and I believe cause a loss of joy for God. Like Krystal, we forget that God loves us best, and allow ourselves to go to a place of despair. Many times I think we ruin opportunities that the Lord has set up for Him and us to spend quality time together because we refuse to look upon our gifts with adoration. Many times I think we get stuck looking at what someone else has with God and believe that ours is somehow less than. Then, because we are stuck in our thinking, we refuse to even try out a gift that we feel is inferior. I know when I am reminded of this Christmas, many times I am stopped in my tracks. God only has good gifts for us and He does have them for us. But whether we open and use them or not is up to us.

End notes:

20- **John 14:2,** *In my Father's house are many rooms; if it were not so, I would have told you. I am going there to prepare a place for you.* New International Version

Chapter Six

Helping Me

I think back many times to when Jesus said, "Give me that." I have given a lot of thought to it. That God could come and say that to anyone. Or lets say that God might say "help me", or any statement that He might make to us like this. The truth is that God doesn't need anything. He is God. If by chance there was something that He needed then He could create it. So to say to me "Give me that " in a tone that expresses "help me" is something to think about.

God can do everything without us. So why does He choose to do things with us, or let us do things for someone else when He could just do it Himself and have no problems?

It was wonderful to find out that the God who lives inside of me does help me. The God who lives in me does say, "Give me that". He is very able to get rid of and change all kinds of things for us, and He knows what we need and in what order to do stuff because He is God, and He is inside of us.

The idea that He doesn't understand, because He is out of touch with us is wrong. The pressure to try to explain ourselves to God when we can't explain it to another human, leaves us believing it is hopeless to truly be understood. We begin grappling with what to do with our personal experiences, because God has never had to experience what we are dealing with. This too is wrong. God, through Jesus, did experience, and Jesus is the only man who is capable of judging mankind. He knows because He lived and lives inside of us through the Holy Spirit. He is a God of great experience, and the truth is that He understands us better than we understand ourselves. If we are in the process of trying to obtain understanding, it is because He, Jesus, wants us to know something that He feels we need revelation on. All true revelation comes from God.

He knows what we feel, the frustration, and the shame. He knows our joy, and happiness. He knows all these things. Not just the dictionary meaning but knowledge from a life that He lived. He rules above us. He can come and get us and help us. He is always a wonderful gentleman and at the same time in perfect unity a fierce protector. Many times He has to protect us from ourselves.

I recall another vision that I had in Kansas City. It was February 2005 and I went to Kansas City with a group of ten women. I had gone to the front of the IHOP to hide. God was moving in the women and they were coming to me with what He was doing.

I cannot tell you how inadequate I felt. Knowing my life and my pain I didn't want to misrepresent God or give bad advice. So I hid. The ladies were expecting me to meet them at a prearranged time for all of us to go and meet the prophets and receive a prophetic word. Since I kind of set the plan in motion they related to me as the leader of the group. Being a leader should be taken serious and it was scaring the day lights out of me.

So I went to hide in the front row of the IHOP. I hid my face in the back of the chairs by laying down. Unless you walked to the front row you would not have guessed that I was up there. I was talking to God about the ladies, and how unequipped I was. The next thing I remember I was on a hillside. There was a wide white platform up on the top of a knoll. On it stood Jesus. He was wearing what looked like a white suit. There were a lot of people at the gathering. They also were all in white. I want to take a minute and tell you about their clothes. People were dressed how they might be today except all the clothes were made out of the same material. It was the material my dress had been made out of when I danced with Jesus in the castle. It was lightweight and flowing. It looked beautiful on every single person.

Jesus was standing with a couple of big angels. He asked, "Where is she?"

I just knew He was looking at me. In my mind I could see myself as well. I don't know how this is possible because there was no mirror around, but I knew exactly what I looked like. When I looked down at myself I was so shocked and horrified. I was wearing a very trashy, sleazy, red dress. It had a terrible rose pinned just above my belly button. The dress was too small and very unflattering to my figure and my coloring. I hated the dress! I never looked so fat, or frumpy, or indecent. The dress was a halter dress which leaves the back open. But the back exposed too much, and the slit on the side came up much too high. The front was two pieces of material that started at the waist and went up around the neck. It was so skimpy that my breasts were barely covered. It was the most horrible dress I have ever seen on a lady. I knew I have never in all my outfits ever looked so badly. I just wanted to disappear. I can never remember feeling so badly about myself.

My hair was "Big". I grew up in the 1980's so big hair is my favorite, but not the big hair I was wearing. This hair looked like it was a bird nest stuck on top of my head. My makeup was as dramatic as a person's makeup performing in a play, and so over exaggerated. I had a terrible amount of perfume on, and heavy earrings. I also was wearing the worst spike shoes. Everything about my outfit was wrong for me, and wrong for where I was.

Jesus asked again to the crowd "Where is she?"

The crowd split and there was an open pathway right to me. I panicked. I was so upset as He walked toward me. He was breathtaking in His entire splendor. I was terrified and in utter shame.

As Jesus walked toward me so did His angels. There was no place for me to escape to, or hide in. His eyes were fixed on me and nothing was diverting

His attention from me. I knew all of me, all my shame, was exposed.

Jesus reached out His hand to take a hold of my hand. I stepped back and said in a screechy sounding voice, "No Lord, don't touch me!" And I desperately tried to cover the front of my body with my arms folded across my chest as my eyes tried hard not to look at His beauty.

Jesus strongly asked a question of me "What are the charges!"

Answers started pouring out of my being. I started with: "I am a prostitute!" I know I must have moved on the chairs I was laying on. Everything felt my answer, my physical body, my spiritual body, and my emotional body. I was so undone and radically dissected.

I hated that truth! I couldn't believe I had given Jesus an answer like that. I never have physically been a prostitute in the earthly meaning of one. But in heavens eyes many times I have physically let someone use me for some money, or recognition. Emotionally I have many times been in the act of prostitution and spiritually with God, I have given myself to ways that I knew were against God. But to actually say it in front of Jesus was so shocking and scary. I was standing before Him exposed as to what I was.

I lifted my eyes and watched Him nod His head at me. It was terrible to have His agreement and at the same time so freeing.

He asked again "What are the charges?"

More and more poured out of me. I remember telling Him things like: "I don't believe you are whom you say you are or that you can do what you say you can do. I do not believe I am who you say I am or that you could really love me with that everlasting fierce love that is as strong as death. I don't believe you love mankind. I don't believe you'll bring me to heaven with you or that you would never leave me. I don't believe that the power of God is in me, or in the world. I don't believe!"

Again I started a new onslaught of exposing. "I am a thief, a murderer, and a liar. I am a slanderer, a false witness, and a bitter woman. I am a covetous woman, and wicked." Each time I made a statement I felt such pain, rejection and shame. Each time I felt like I was free from the weight of ugly secrets. Each time, Jesus nodded his brilliant head at me and waited for the rest.

Finally I had no more in me. I had shown Him every terrible ugly thing in me physically, emotionally, and spiritually. He had a total picture of who I really am.

I was sure that I had His undivided attention. Jesus was not going anywhere. He was so patient to let me explain everything and His question demanded that I answer it in its entirety. He was going to hear everything and see everything and sense everything. As I confessed my experiences He too relived them.

I looked at Jesus the whole time. This surprised me. I would have thought that I would have had enough sense to look down in my shame, but I looked Him in the eye.

When I was finished, Jesus smiled at me and picked up my hands and placed them between His hands. I couldn't believe it! He stood looking at me with adoring eyes.

He said, "Yes, all of these charges were true, and they were true before I saved you. Laurie, you are the only one who can see those charges. You can leave the shame now and come with me." He was so gentle so caring, so loving. His patience and acceptance was Holy.

I looked down and I was wearing a beautiful white gown. I looked very beautiful. He put out His left arm for me to walk with Him, the way I imagine a King would for a Queen. We began walking down the aisle that had been cleared when He had first called out "Where is she?" I never felt so clean, so pure and holy. As I walked with Him I understood that I needed to give Him my shame, I needed to give Him my pain. When He saved me He took a lot of the yuck and pain away, but there was still stuff that He needed to take for me to be His Bride. I understood that guilt says you did the wrong thing, shame says you are the wrong thing.

Shame will keep you away from God and will torture you. Jesus truly wants us set free. As we walked I felt His love for me race through my whole body. When we reached the two Angels that were standing waiting for Him, He turned to me and said something that shocked me and drew me out of the vision.

Jesus looked at me and said "Thank-you".

Can you believe this?

Upon awaking from this vision I noticed the time. It was time to go with the women of our group into the prophetic rooms and meet with the prophets.

As we sat waiting I pondered the vision, especially the part about Jesus saying "Thank-you" to me. Since then, I have told this vision to people and the verdict is split on whether they believe it or not. I try not to say things on purpose that cause division with my fellow believers, this one does though. That God would thank people has upset many I relate this vision to.

When it came for my turn to go in and meet with the prophets, the confirmation came when one of the lady prophets said to me is that she senses Jesus is saying "Thank-you" over me. It's a good thing they give you the tape of what they are saying over you because I had to listen to it a few times to believe in this realm that He had really said that to me.

It is amazing still that Jesus would ask for people like us to be with Him in His Kingdom. That He would ask anything and not demand everything. That He would say let me help you, or give me that, or thank-you. But this is the Jesus who has shown Himself to me. This is the same Jesus who commands demons to flee and the wind to stop. I am sure I do not know Him well enough, but I am positive that I want to.

There are a couple more visions I want to share. Visions where there is an understanding of God's ability to Judge. See, It is true that Jesus is patient, but He still is God. He is the Judge and all of His judgments are righteous.

There was a vision I had where I was standing before God in His private judge chambers. He was so powerful. He was dressed the way I think an old English Judge might be dressed. In like a military uniform, but I had never seen a uniform like the one that God was wearing. The buttons on His uniform shinned so brightly that the shine hid the color of the whole uniform. Each button represented what I might refer to as a pin or medal of great and highest honor. His honor was so big that nothing could contain it so a button represented it. No man on the earth has ever received so many honors as to even wear one of these buttons. But God had so many honors that there were many buttons on His suit. They were so bright that I could hardly see anything else but His honor.

He had powerful white hair. There is no under-standing in me either as to why the white hair was powerful, but I do know that even the hair of God showed the extent of His majesty. So the white hair was very significant. The color white, although this white is every color mixed perfectly together, its creation is in itself wisdom, knowledge, and revelation. He knew everything of the past, present, and future. This truth was explained in the very fibers of His hair.

Inside His chamber room there is no noise. No noise because only His words are needed. I believe this is important because He knew everything, the questions and the answers.

He called me to Him. As I stood by Him I could smell Him. I know this sounds strange if you have never heard of God having a smell before. But He had convinced me of this sense of smell in our world a different time when I had been at the One Thing. (The One Thing is a conference that the IHOP puts on for young adults. It is one of the most powerful events I have attended. The speakers there love Jesus and have a incredible way of sharing and showing that love to the ten thousand plus young adults that are attending.) Now I know that I am not a young adult according to the world, still the event is for all, it is just geared for the younger ones. By the way, unless there is a height requirement, never be so prideful to think that God can't teach you something that He is sharing with the younger ones.

I was watching a band at the One Thing conference and they were piping in some smoke and with the smoke came the most wonderful powerful smell. It was so unique, but at the same time it was strangely familiar. I asked the man next to me if he could smell that smell and he said it was the "fragrance of the Lord". I liked it so much I went out to the bookstore and told the lady by the candle display that I wanted to buy the "fragrance of the Lord". She explained that they sold myrrh and frankincense, but that the "fragrance of the Lord" is not for sale. She went on after my complaining to explain that this fragrance is for real. There is a real fragrance of God. When He shows up you can really smell Him. I did not believe her. It was ridiculous to me to even try to think that God had His own smell.

The clerk explained that in His presence there are also smells. So I went down to the basement floor of the same building as the bookstore and found the closest bathroom. Once inside I checked to see that I was alone in the restroom. Then out loud I said: "God, if you want me to believe this whole 'fragrance of the Lord' thing your going to have to prove it to me. Make this bathroom be a place of your presence."

There was no waiting. The whole room filled with the smell. Talk about experiencing the 'fear of the Lord'! I wanted out of the bathroom so quick I was tripping over myself to get upstairs and tell Mike that the smell thing was for real.

As I stood by the Judge in my vision with the white hair and shining coat noticing His smell I also noticed that God's eyes were blazing. Not a scary 'run and hide' blaze, but a full and steady blaze that was most comforting. Next He asked me without spoken words if I could let Him hold my pain. I didn't know how to let Him, but I understood that He was capable of holding it if I were capable of giving it. I just wasn't sure how to give it.

Then God replayed a painful memory of my past where someone important to me spits on me. Not an accidental spray while conversing, but an intentional display of worthlessness. It is a very painful and degrading thing to be spit on, and God was concentrating on this pain in my life.

If this has ever happened to you then you can relate to the shame and humiliation that covers your life. If no one removes this shame, it becomes very hard to remove it on your own. God knows this, and as a Judge, He has a way to fix it.

So He showed me how to give it to Him. Again, He used a vision to help me grasp what I could not understand on my own.

I was crying in front of God the Judge; my make-up was running down my face and severely smeared around my eyes. He took the sleeve of His beautiful coat/robe and wiped my face. I could see the color of the coat now and not just the shine of the honor. The color of His uniform was a magnificent white. Not any white, but a white that holds all the colors ever made. There is no white on earth like it. On earth white is a color you start with, then add other colors to get something. Not so with God. His white is perfection. It is what is achieved when all things reach their full potential in perfection.

He wiped my face so gently with His right hand that was partially covered with the coat. The Gentleness of God was so life giving that I physically felt the pain of the spit being removed. Then I looked at His robe. There was the stain of my pain and shame carried by my tears and make-up smeared on the most perfect piece of clothing and on the most powerful judge ever. It could be seen. This terrible stain had diminished the shine of even the magnificent buttons. The stain covered the brilliant white and did not belong on the Judge's perfection.

I didn't want Him to have my shame, it looked so badly on Him, on His clothes, on His life, and before I could begin to complain I heard Him speak without words to my heart that 'this was very good'.

The Judge wanted me to know that this was very good. To let Him carry the pain and shame was very good. He was proud of me. I didn't understand, so God, as a Judge, told me His reason for doing it.

I was unable to carry this pain. It was something that had come to steal, kill, and destroy my life. The Bible [21]says that the enemy of God wants to do this, steal, kill, and destroy us. But God won't stand by and just let it happen, He is for us. So when I let

God carry my shame, it sets me free. Then I understood that the stain of my pain would be a constant reminder to God that my situation was very serious. For the stain to be removed from His robe one of two things had to happen. Either the person who had spit on me would have to ask for forgiveness from their heart, God would know if they meant it, or God would remove the stain on Judgment day.

Either way, God would deal with the stain. I have nothing to do with it except say "Father, forgive them because they didn't know that you would carry the pain and shame and that they were really spitting on you."

Many times I have to remember this vision and try to get myself before God in His chambers and give Him my pain. It only happened once that God played out the scenario for me, but each time I struggle I try to remember what He showed me. I don't like the pain to be on God, but the only other option is to let the pain steal, kill or destroy my life and I know this would be worse for God than the stain to be on His perfection. Forgiveness doesn't mean that what happened is alright, and you try to forget it and ignore the pain. Forgiveness means that you trust God to do what is best and you give Him the pain.

There was another vision I had about God and His ability to Judge. I want to share this vision here so that I balance out what God has taught me on His justice. In the vision I was in a building that might be similar to football stadium. It held a lot of people and everything looked down to the center where God held His court. I was in the front center about halfway up between the court floor and the top seats. Jesus was sitting at a big desk conducting His business. There were two angels standing with Him. They did not look like I thought an angel would look like. They looked like big, strong men. But in the vision I knew they were His angels. God looked like the vision I had of Him as a Judge with the white hair and the beautiful coat. He talked with one of His angels, and the angel nodded and left His side.

The same angel was standing at my side almost immediately and asked me a question "Are you sure you want to meet the Lord in His courtroom, or would you prefer His private chambers?"

I explained that no, I would wait here. I needed to see the Lord because He had told me that He would defend me on an issue that was so big and messy. One word from Him and everything would have been fine, but that word had not yet come. I wanted Him to speak on my behalf. I wanted to remind Him of what He had said so that the big mess my life was in would disappear. I sat to watch the courtroom of the Lord. The angel returned to the side of the Lord.

In the room there was a few people waiting to speak with the Lord. Not many at all considering the size of the building.

A woman approached the Lord and He asked her "What are the Charges?"

Before she could speak, the whole building was filled with people. There were so many people that the building had standing room only. The Lord looked at the people and released those who live in forgiveness. Much of the room disappeared but there were still a lot of people in the room. Maybe a third of the seats were filled. It was significantly less than what had just been, but still a huge witness to hear the charges of the woman.

As she spoke, in a language I did not understand, I noticed people would disappear as they were talked about. Finally the Lord nodded His head and all the people including the woman disappeared and there was a great sense of loss and pain inside the room.

The Lord took a minute to regroup and look at the next man waiting for his turn to speak with Him. Before the Lord began with this man His eyes met mine. Again He spoke with the angel who appeared standing by my side.

Again the angel questioned me. "Are you sure you want to meet the Lord in His courtroom, or would you prefer His private chambers?" This time I thought about it, I couldn't remember why, but I knew something about the private chambers of the Lord.

Then the angel spoke again. "He would rather meet you in His private chambers!"

I thought "Oh, good. I can come back here later."

The angel led me, although just agreeing was the engine that moved me to the quiet room of God. Jesus was already waiting for me, The Jesus who loves me, who looked like the diamond man. When I got there He held me and the angel was not present anymore.

Jesus said without words "Laurie, I never want to see you in my courtroom." I didn't understand.

Jesus said again with so much gentleness into my heart "Laurie, I never, ever, want to see you in my courtroom again." I still did not understand.

I knew that this was so important, but I did not understand. I did not understand the importance of what Jesus was telling me. I became very afraid. In the presence of Jesus I was very afraid.

Some people have told me that this vision could not have been a real vision from God because of this fear, but I strongly disagree. I was so afraid because I did not understand the direct words from Jesus to me. I know that when Jesus speaks it is so important. If we do not live our lives on His words and His meanings we will perish. I was so fearful of perishing.

I could feel the love of Jesus as His arms were around me. I could hear the love of Jesus in the gentle tones He spoke into my heart. I could see the love of Jesus in His eyes for me. Still I was very afraid to know that the something I did not understand could end this and I could perish.

I have never been so fearful. Ever. I asked Him to help me. Then I received the wisdom and began to understand what the Lord meant.

In the courtroom of the Lord, He Judges wrongs… all wrongs. When someone comes to see the Lord in His courtroom they are expecting Him to judge fairly, and there is no other way for Him to judge. When the people stand before the Lord, He brings all the people associated with that person into His presence. This is because a situation today may be a result from something before hand or have been influenced from someone before hand. We may also use the same results and influence someone after the fact. But the Lord knows all this and brings everyone associated with the life into His presence. This means everyone stands before the Lord when we want justice.

Right away the people who lived their life in forgiveness got to leave. Now over two thirds of the people in the room got to leave. (There were people standing everywhere not just seated in the seats. This means that the people who do live in forgiveness out number the people who don't. It is a lie of the enemy to think that Jesus' ways are not winning. Or that the ways of the enemy, unforgiveness, is the way that most of the people live.)

The ones left seated in the building heard the woman and her reason for needing judgment. Then Jesus judged the people. In the end, all the people, including the woman herself, who did not live their lives in forgiveness received judgment in the court-room of the Lord. It was very sad. They were all punished. They were all sentenced. They were all cast away from Him. This is terrible! This is so scary! I was in that courtroom; God could have sentenced me. I could have been cast away. The only saving thing for me was that I did not play a part in the life of the woman. On the day that I was there though, I too held resentment and unforgiveness. I wanted justice, and if He had needed to judge me, I would have perished.

He wants to bring us to His private chambers where instead of justice and judgment we can receive mercy and grace. Where we can leave pain with Him to deal with in such a way that will keep us safe. I understood that if I chose judgment before God, He would judge me too. Even though I am the one that He loves, He would judge me.

I was so scared. And I hope I have explained it in such a way that it scares you too. You never want to be in the courtroom of the Lord when He is dealing out His justice. You will get what you deserve. Instead, live your life in forgiveness and run to Him in His private chambers where He will fix the problem. Maybe not in our understanding of time, but it will be fixed.

I also never want to send anyone to the court-room of God and have their life judged. I pray that if I ever end up there that I am one of the ones that live in forgiveness and are allowed to disappear right away. It hurt Jesus to Judge the people and the pain was physically felt in the room. But as the Judge, He will perform this aspect of Himself perfectly. It's cost is always an expense to Him. I never want to hurt Him that way.

We have the time right now to get to know the Jesus who would say, "let me help you", or "thank-you", or even "give me that". We can also meet the Judge who loves us and wants us to live in forgiveness.

This same Jesus is also a Judge who said ***"Yes, if you forgive others for their sins, your Father in heaven will also forgive you for your sins. But if you don't forgive others, your Father in heaven will not forgive your sins."*** **Matthew 6:14-15** New Century Version

End notes:

21- **John 10:10,** *A thief comes to steal and kill and destroy, but I came to give life- life in all its fullness.* New Century Version

Chapter Seven

Set Me Free

The patience of God, as one of the fruits of the Spirit is such a beautiful thing. I try to be patient, but it is nothing compared to the real patience of God. He is so patient with us and loves us so much. But in turmoil it is very hard to believe this. For me all God has to do is tell me "Laurie, you are being the hummingbird".

I wonder many times why God doesn't just force Himself on us and do for us what is best, but He doesn't. Many times it is because we are as hummingbirds.

I am someone who learns best with hands on applications. I will remember almost anything you show me if you let me do it. I can turn right around and teach what I just learned using the "show me" method. I have often told many during my teaching times that I am not a real teacher, just a really good student. I can show you what I learned.

Secondly, I learn best by listening to what you are saying while taking notes. I can do this with a video too, but I prefer being at the conference. Then I like to go and discuss what I heard. It is almost like I quickly give it away, using the let "me show you" method.

Thirdly, I hardly learn anything if I read it.

God made me this way. He knows how I am and why I am like I am. He likes that I am an experiencing person. He likes that I have to do it or live it, to understand it. If you are this way, I want you to know that He likes that in you too.

I have heard it said many times that we should not ask God for experiences. I disagree...strongly! The Lord has taught me many things by letting me experience it. It is like telling the child "God is good." This may be, but if they don't experience good, then God only is. And they could misunderstand what is good, and who is God. So God Himself sets up situations to show them that He is good and they can believe.

As I write down these experiences I pray that they might help you experience God in new ways. That everyone can know that God is good and that He has situations that He sets up to give us hands on "show me" experiences. And that all you have to do is say "Yes!"

This is my hummingbird experience. It was during one of my most mixed up times that God came to help me. If He had been talking there was no way that I could have been hearing Him so He set up an experience for me.

Have you ever been frustrated beyond description? I know this! I have experienced this and there are not words to explain how frustrated I was on this one spring day. I had been frustrated for a week or more coming up to this day. So this was probably one of the most frustrating time periods I can remember.

It was Sunday morning. I woke up late to a dirty kitchen (Frustration). The girls hadn't hustled to get to church so we were running late (Frustration). My husband, Mike, was reading his Bible and not helping straighten up the kitchen (Frustration). When we got to church the person I had gotten to replace me at the greeting center had not and I was being questioned(Frustration). Many people wanted to share about their week while I was trying to quickly fix the information center (Frustration). The Pastor seemed to talk to long (Frustration). There was nothing at home for lunch (Frustration). On the ride home everyone was talking about how wonderful the service had been (Frustration). I just WANTED TO SCREAM!

I said, "How can everyone be so happy? There is nothing to be so happy about!" I said it so forcefully that I instantly quieted the car. My family did not want to be around me, nor did I want to be around them. They filed out of the car and I was so upset and frustrated that I just knew I was going to blow my lid. I could feel the shaking going on inside myself, so much frustration. Everyone went into the house and I remained in the garage.

Then I noticed the humming bird and heard the sound of it hitting against the glass on the inside of the garage window. It seems that the bird had found its way into our garage and could only see one way out. It was so focused on getting out through the glass that it wasn't even searching the room to see that the huge garage door was wide open.

"Stupid bird!" I thought.

And it just kept on hitting the glass.

I remembered the conversation on the ride home, "There are many things to be happy about!" my husband corrected me right before he got out of the car. Frustration! I was so upset and angry that I did not go inside with them. Instead I paced in my garage. The shaking inside me was so great. Should I cry? Should I fight with someone? Should I get in the car and drive far away?

"Why? " I kept asking God. " Why this? Why me? Why now?" And the bird kept hitting the glass. "Stupid Bird!" I said out loud.

Then I looked at it. It was a baby humming bird. Hadn't I always loved to watch the humming birds and especially the very small ones? So what! I was not in any mind set to watch this bird and its beauty but…

All right. It needed help or it was going to smash its brains into the glass. Since I was the only person in the garage it had to be me who was going to help the stupid bird. Or I was going to have to go inside and ask for help.

I went and put on my husbands thick hard leather gloves. They were big and bulky around my hands. Too big to be used as gloves but I didn't want to take the time to find my soft, snug gloves. I was in a bad fit. You know how it is when your seatbelt isn't snug? You're not prepared for a sudden stop, so you're in a bad fit. You're not using the right technique but your expecting the right results.

Then I marched over to the bird. I was just about to grab it in my anger when something stopped me. It was like time stood still for a second. Sometimes this feeling is coldness somewhere or a caution in your spirit. I like to believe it is God screaming "HEY!" just to get your attention.

This beautiful creature was frantic. It was trapped. It could see where it needed to be but it could not get there. Freedom was so close but some invisible force (a real window glass pane) had created a prison. It was frustrated. It had entered a state of panic and reason was not available anymore. It was killing itself. In some strange way, I could relate.

I put my hands out to grab the bird and realized that the gloves in themselves could harm the tiny bird. I flicked the leather to the ground. I attempted to place my hands around the bird but realized if I touched it I would mortally harm its beautiful deli-cate wings, wings that were frantic. I had to do some-thing and I needed to do something smart. I cupped my hands underneath the bird and it almost instantly collapsed, flopping down on its wing and landing right in my hands.

I thought it was dead. I thought it had hit its head one to many times and had killed itself. I started to cry.

"What if?" I thought. "What if I had been nicer? Or had hurried and ran for help? Or had tried to grab it sooner?" My heart hurt that this little bird had basically died right in my hands.

Then I saw its eye move. It was such a tiny eye that looked like a speck of pepper. There was an eye there and then there wasn't. It would open and then it would close again. I was so excited and I started to pray over it. It barely moved but I could see its little belly slightly expand as it breathed. It was exhausted. I was so thankful I had been there to catch it just in enough time.

Then I understood what God was trying to tell me. Suddenly I knew. I understood God. I am just like this bird!

I am the bird. I am so frantic I can't see another way out so I keep hitting my head against an invisible wall. He wants to help me but He can't grab me or I could hurt myself. He has to just wait with His hands poised under me to catch me when I fall.

I stood there looking at one of the most beautiful creatures and crying and thanking God that He had chosen me to catch this baby. It was very humbling to know that in my frantic, uncaring state God had chosen me. He could use me even in that state.

As I walked out to the back porch my husband came out to check on me.

I showed him the beautiful hummingbird. It was amazing to be holding a bird, let alone a quick little hummingbird. It was one of those God moments, when you know that you know that unless the hand of God, none of this would be happening. Then I explained to Mike what God had explained to me. Mike agreed I am the hummingbird. I had been frantic for so long.

I was trapped and so desperate that I couldn't hear God, or Mike, or our girls reaching out to help me.

As I went to sit down at our picnic table I knew it was time to let the little bird go. As God let me hold it until it was at peace and strong enough to fly, so He had been holding me so that I could experience it and be at peace and be strong. I opened my hands wide and it just flew away.

God had caught me, had given me a time to regroup, or understand, and like the bird He was setting me free. I have remembered this experience many times since then. It has taught me time and time again how I need to try to look around and try to find the wide-open garage door to get out of my problem. Many times God has had to wait for me to collapse before He can set me free.

Maybe He is waiting for you to collapse so He can set you free too. If so, be thankful that He is so patient. Jesus knows us so well and He will take His time to bring us to a clear understanding that He is so patient.

Chapter Eight

Do whatever it takes.

I don't know if using visions to explain a vision is politically correct, or in this case religiously correct, but many times this is how Jesus shows me what is needed in my life.

In the vision where Jesus asked me to give Him my cigarette smoking I remember believing that I was so important to Jesus. As I watched me dance with Jesus I believed I was the woman He would lay down His life for. That He would do what ever it takes to protect me, even unto death. Nothing was going to separate me from Him and He would use His life and His very blood to protect me. He says this in the Bible too: **Romans 8:38-39,** *Yes, I am sure that neither death, nor life, nor angels, nor ruling spirits, nothing now, nothing in the future, no powers, nothing above us, nothing below us, nor anything else in the whole world will ever be able* *to separate us from the love of God that is in Christ Jesus our Lord.* New Century Version.

When you own this, you can be a radical follower of Jesus. I had the vision, but I know I am not yet who Jesus can transform me to be. There is nothing that is going to stop Him from protecting you if you follow him. Honestly, I do not use this as often as I need. I know that I know that this is true, but often times I forget.

There was another time when I was at IHOP at a One Thing Conference, when God showed me something wonderful through something terrible. I want to take a minute and tell you again that if it is possible to get to a One Thing Conference, go! They are life changing.

My family had gone to the first One Thing Conference, that caused amazing and radical changes to happen in each of our lives. When we came back I sold the youth group leader on taking our group, or as many as could save up enough money down the next year. I told everyone I could about the One Thing. The following year there were twenty-five of us that went there. Our youth group and a college group from a town close by combined to form one big group. Let me tell you, it cost us something to get there. Meeting God in a new way sometimes does. This time, it cost us some money and some other things we didn't want to carry around.

At the conference there were some mini breakout sessions. There was one being taught by a man named Stuart. I chose his session because I had heard him the year before and had really enjoyed his teaching.

Stuart is a powerful and gifted man of God. Many people attended this session and I was sitting with the youth group leader, and two others from our group. Up ahead about ten rows sat my husband, Mike, and another of the college men.

Stuart started teaching, and there seemed to be something going on in the spirit realm that might be different than what we were hearing. Suddenly, the atmosphere in the whole room changed. Stuart stated that the Holy Spirit was there. Boy oh boy was the Holy Spirit ever there. Stuart said that they needed to pray for the missionaries. Many young people stood up to get into line. It was amazing to me that the majority of the room were people who felt that being a missionary was in their future. Stuart started asking the Lord to mark them. To mark the ones in the room that God had big plans for.

I got drawn into a vision on two realms at the same time. I could see the young people in line and at the same time, a vision of what their lives were going to go through. Nothing has ever deeply hurt me so much. As I tell this, I want to also tell you that all the things of God are not always pleasant. Sometimes the visions will hurt.

I looked at the line and noticed that the kids had a red glow around them. It was kind of like the white glow that is painted on the Christmas cards over baby Jesus' head. This red glow went around the people though. It jumped out maybe 6 inches from their bodies and started at just below the left shoulder and went up around their heads and down to the right shoulder. I tried to refocus my eyes but the glow stayed put.

I had experienced the red glow in a different way the year before. I was in a breakout secession when a young man who said that the 'red light of revelation' was in the room. This light was there to help us. I did not see the red light, but went along with the bow your head thing just in case this new strange thing was God.

It was! The man speaking said to ask God what He was wanting to do. Then the man said to ask Jesus, "what is it that hurts (put your name here) the most?" I did. I got this answer running across my mind as if a ticker tape was playing.

WHAT HURTS LAURIE DITTO THE MOST IS......LAURIE DITTO BELIEVES......LAURIE DITTO IS STUPID!

Then the man told us to allow the Lord to come and minister to us in the area that He was working in. Then a crazy thing happened. As my head was bowed over my knees a light shined into my right eye. It was like when I was a child I would place a flashlight over my eye in the dark, almost identical in fact. I could feel my whole right side of my brain light up. It was strange, but it didn't hurt. I tried to play a game with the light to get it to move over to the side, but it was stuck. I listened as the man prayed and I agreed with everything. He prayed wonderful things that were uplifting. Then I felt something move inside of me. It was like God pulled out all the stuff out of my brain that He knew was hurting me and causing me to believe lies. I felt things, like strings being pulled out of me. It felt as if a piece of silk was being removed. I was a little disoriented, but an amazing thing had happened. The 'red light of revelation' had helped me tremendously.

Back in the breakout session where Stuart was teaching he kept saying: "Mark them Lord!" And as he said this more and more of the young people standing in line ended up with the red glow around them. I believe this was the same 'red light of revelation'.

Suddenly, as I was looking at the young people in line, I could see something terrible happen to them. I will pick a few just to explain what I was seeing. There was a girl standing in line. Maybe she was fifteen years old. In the vision I was seeing her older than she was currently, much older I think. She was in a dark alleyway somewhere. There were mean and angry men all around her. They kept yelling and pushing her and spitting on her. She was on her knees in front of one man who was screaming at her in a language I did not know. She was holding both of her hands high in the air, the way you do when you worship God. This made the man very angry. He tried to force her arms down but the arms stayed high. The man took a big machete knife and cut off one of her arms. Blood shot everywhere. I started screaming and crying. The girl in the vision picked up her cut stub of an arm and continued to praise God.

It caused a severe and extreme unsettling deep in the core of me! The people sitting with me had no idea what was going on. I dropped on the chairs right to the floor. They were trying to console me when I heard God ask me if He could give me more. I don't think I answered yes, but I saw another one.

In the line was a couple. Maybe they were a couple already, but in the vision they were husband and wife and much older than they were in the room. Something bad was happening. She was also down on her knees, hurt, tied up, sweaty, bleeding on her face, and something stuck in her mouth. Angry men were yelling at the husband. I understood their language, but what they were saying made no sense to me. They were yelling "Now traitor! Now!" And they were waving guns, big guns. The man looked down at his wife and she shook her eyes as if to say "no". The angry man put the gun to the girls' head and shot her dead. I watched! It was one of the most real things I have ever experienced.

I cannot tell you the pain my physical body was going through. It was so real, so frightening, and so terrible and not like anything I had ever seen. I am not a guts and gory kind of girl, just the opposite. I can't watch movies like that.

It happened many times and although I could not stand to look at the people, I knew I had to. I prayed: "God, don't show me any of our kids in our group, not one." He did not.

I looked up front. I saw Mike. He had a glow around him, and I saw things that made me very proud of him and very angry at the same time. I wept and wept. I knew there was no way for me to leave the room. I was never going to ever feel joy again. What ever was happening in the room had left me in a total sense of hopelessness and despair.

I felt the Lord ask me if He could give me more. I figured I was going to die right there. I said, "yes" because I didn't know how I could live with all the gory graphics I had just seen. Or how I could ever let Mike be who I had seen him be. "Yes".

I saw myself. I was in a hot place. I was sweating all over. There was a lot of dirt, and funny little bushes. The man was pulling me around by my hair and there were lots of little kids around. There were very angry men and they wanted me to say a certain phrase. They kept repeating it to me over and over. Every time they said it I shook my head 'no'. Someone would pull my hair and slap my face. I heard a lot of people crying and there was a lot of fear. A man put a gun up to my mouth and another man opened my mouth. It was very intense.

Suddenly, everything froze. I remember hearing my breath and that was the only sound I could hear. I figured I was dead. I could feel my heart beating so fast and my breath didn't feel like my own.

I looked out past the frozen man in front of me, and a man was walking towards me. It was kind of like a mirage. A man in white pants and a white tunic long sleeved shirt was walking towards me. Somehow I ended up in front of this man in white, while everything else stayed frozen.

It was Jesus. He was beautiful. He held me and I knew everything was going to be all right. First, I let Him hold me until I had caught my breath and then, I began telling Him everything that was happening. His smile was amazing and filled with adoration. He nodded each time I took a breath. Jesus is very interested in what we have to say. I continued on and on until I felt I had given a full report of a terrible unsettling situation. Again He nodded.

I appreciate the utter patience of Jesus. The Bible says that He is long suffering, but I am not sure we understand what that means. I often thought that long suffering meant that He would tolerate us. Maybe He would be standing bored over us knowing what we are going to say and impatient that we talk too slow for Him. I used to think that God was stuck listening to gibberish that was a repeat for Him since He knows everything anyway. My mind returns to elementary school where the teacher was repeating a lesson that I already knew. I used to daydream out the window and wait for her to be finished talking so that I could get on with what was important to me.

That may have been how I was, but that is not how God is. Jesus never looked sorry that He was listening to me. Never in a vision that I have had, has He ever been a daydreamer. We are important to Him, with an importance that is Supernatural.

The only importance I can relate it to is the importance of a newborn. I remember when the nurse handed me each of our daughters. They really weren't doing anything that was extremely unique or exceedingly special, but just because they "are" was mesmerizing to me. I wanted to watch every breath they took. I wanted to hear every sound and fix every little problem they might have. To a degree, it is still this way for me with my family. They are so important and when I keep my priorities straight, they remain world-renowned important to me. When my priorities get messed up, I get bored with them.

I know that Jesus always, always, keeps His priorities straight and we are extremely important to Him. Many times in my daily walk He has to remind me of this so that I can keep Him a priority and stay spiritually connected. I would think it should never be a problem keeping priorities straight. But it is. The only thing I can take credit for is that when I find myself off track, I ask Him to help me. I don't always feel like doing what is necessary to get re-connected, but if I just remember who Jesus is it becomes much easier. I think about what He has done for me, and how grateful I need to be. I am grateful to God, but many times I need to remind myself to be grateful.

Anyway, after I had explained everything to Jesus about the bad guys, the anger, the fear, and the terrible situation. He gave me a look that let me know that everything was gong to be all right. Have you ever had a look like that from someone else?

In a place of great turmoil, someone looks at you and you just know that everything is going to be all right. Like when a loving Grandfather puts his arm around you and says, "Don't worry child, everything will turn out all right." It is like a new strength comes in you. As if just explaining it with your mouth, hearing it with your ears, and seeing with your eyes acceptance from another set of eyes enables you to accomplish another round.

I could believe Jesus. Everything was going to be alright. I was ready to step back into time and not be afraid, no matter what was going to happen to me. I knew it was going to be powerful and that since Jesus was there, I could do it. I could tell even these mean people about Him, and no matter what, everything was going to be fine.

Jesus had a different plan. He intended for me to walk away and for Him to stand there and let the bad guys hurt Him.

"No, No Jesus!" I kept arguing with Him. It was enough for Him to step into the trouble and strengthen me, to remove my fear, but it would be wrong for Jesus to be hurt. He is perfect, loving, much to valuable and precious to be killed.

There it was. Killed. That is what the situation's outcome was going to be. I sensed it and so did Jesus. Those angry, violent men were going to kill me. Jesus was going to die in my place.

"No, No Jesus!", I kept repeating as I tried to pull Him into the direction He had walked from. But He wasn't moving. His eyes understood. He knew that I loved Him, and that I definitely had the strength to stand and let the bad guys kill me, but I couldn't bare to let it be my Jesus.

He reminded me, not in spoken words, but His heart talking to my heart. That this is what He did for me at the cross. The difference was that I didn't understand it at first. He had died for me, even though I would not have died for Him and didn't appreciate it for most of my life.

He said, "You go on now, up over the hill there." He motioned with His eyes the direction for me to go in. Then in heart to heart understanding I received the revelation that: No one can take my life from me, it's

God's. He paid for it He owns it. Jesus knew exactly where I was, and what was going on, and He would protect me, unto death.

If the bad guys came to the saving knowledge of Jesus and asked for forgiveness for killing me, He could forgive them, because they really killed Him.

Wow, What a peace came over me. Everybody knows that you can't kill Jesus. He beat death. So if they shoot Him, nothing changes. I started to walk away and quickly turned back, was this right? Is it so easy to miss death? I looked again at Jesus who was so patiently waiting for me to get to a safe distance before He let the bullet hit Him.

I jolted out of the vision. I was still in the room where Stuart was teaching. Where he was praying for people. I was so filled with shock. I had no grid to base this experience on. Nothing like this had ever happened. All my emotions were on high. I shook as if I was cold but I could feel the sweat in my hair. This for me is extreme, because I don't sweat and usually get ill when I do sweat.

I wondered how I was ever going to live my life with all the graphic pictures in my mind. This is when I began to laugh. I laughed and laughed. I laughed for over two hours. It was not a normal laugh. Every time I saw a person with the red glow around them I laughed. To know that Jesus has something so special planned for them made me laugh. It made me laugh to think of all the fear that one body could hold and it be totally swept away with God's ability to control everything.

I laughed and laughed non-stop. I felt pressure and pain leave my body as I laughed. I felt new life enter into me as I laughed.

I have to tell you, my group thought I was a little nutty. No one in our group had ever seen anything like it before. It was not easy to explain. I knew that the people with the red glow were marked people by God who were going to lay down their life for Jesus, but the weird thing is that it is going to be so easy. I would want to be here when the Lord returns but how wonderful and easy it would be to die this way. I just thought it was funny. Funny that even death can not separate us from God.

With each laugh I got stronger. I always thought that the joy of the Lord was an inner thing, not easily seen on the outside. I still believe this, but with a few exceptions now. I believe God did mark the special people that day, and I also believe He equipped them to do what ever it takes to follow him.

It might get hard to tell people about Jesus someday. Harder than just people thinking we are a little extreme. Someday, it might cost a life. It will be alright, He already knows the cost and would never put one of His loved ones in a place where we would be without Him.

Chapter Nine

Be Ready!

J esus told me: "Go tell others about me." I am sure
He meant it. So, I tell what I know about Him, in
the language of "Laurie Ditto". Do I tell everything
right, or perfectly understandable? I'm sure I don't.
I also think trying to tell someone by writing it is a
much bigger and more difficult challenge. But I am
obedient to try. I want to encourage you to do one
of two things: Number one, get to know Jesus, and
number two, tell others what you know about Him.

See, people have wanted me to have a personal
relationship with Jesus all throughout my life. One
of the first people to make a serious point of trying
to "tell" me about Jesus was my Grandfather, "Pap
Pa". He knew his Bible, he believed it, and he tried
to live it. He died when I was young, but I remember
he tried to talk to me using the powerful words of the
Word of God and he quoted many things that I wish
I could remember. I couldn't then grasp the personal

relationship thing. I understood it was very important to my Grandfather and I wanted to please him, but I only knew how to live with obedience or the "law" of God. It was a good start, but what I needed was what so many had tried to tell me. I needed a personal relationship with Jesus. What I needed was to know the "Grace" of Jesus.

Now if you had asked me, I would have answered that I had a personal relationship. I believed that I had one because I desired one. But desire and possession are not the same.

Jesus is Alive! He is real! He is encountering people through the power of the Holy Spirit. He said He would leave the Holy Spirit to help us, to guide us, and to comfort us. Jesus said He would, and He did. It is through the Holy Spirit that Jesus became so real to me. He became my Savior, my Friend, the Lover of my soul. I wanted to obey Him, but more important, I wanted to know Him. I wanted to know His heart. I wanted to feel Him. I needed to know who He is.

What kind of man, let alone the Creator of the heavens and the earth, would lay down His life for somebody like me? Somebody with all my faults, all my haughtiness, all my pride, and all my idolatry.

I cried out to Him that I want to know you, I want a personal relationship with you. He answered that He wants me to know Him.

He wants us to know Him. So, what do we do? How do we get to know him? What does it look like to begin a personal relationship with God? Start with the Word of God, the Bible. Read the Gospels,

Matthew, Mark, Luke & John. Read about Jesus. Find out if you believe Him. Figure out if you believe what He said, what He did. Let His beauty to help people, when no one else can, amaze you. Read about how He loves the ordinary people, the simple people, the sick people , the "losers" and the "less than" types. Follow along and be surprised about what kind of people He calls friends and what kind of people make Him angry.

Ask Him, every time you read the Bible, to help you know Him. Ask Him to meet you and reveal who He is. He will. He is God, and He can do anything! Ask Him to explain the love of His Cross. Let Him show you in His Holy Words the love He has for people, for you. Ask Him if He gave His life for yours. Ask Him if you will die and be cast out without Him.

Ask Him to give to you visions & dreams. Ask Him to take your inner Spirit Man to be with Him while you sleep and teach your inner Spirit Man all the things about the Kingdom of Heaven. Begin and keep on asking Him all kinds of questions. He enjoys when we turn to Him for answers.

Be ready. God will show up. He will use your life and who you are to begin to share His life. He will use your experiences of the past to explain His Kingdom. He will set up encounters with you, because He is radically in love with you.

You will be able to find Him in all kinds of places, all day long. Places as safe as the flowers in the back yard, or the morning sun rise; to places as challenging as a homeless man on a street corner, or a dying friend who doesn't know Jesus. Then, because you know Him, and how much He loves you and the people around you, you will want to tell others about Him.

Use your language and however you put words together to talk to others about this amazing relationship you will have with God. Use your experiences and the situations you are placed in to show others how He can do all things with and for you. Use your life and all that you are to begin to explain that God loves you, and wants the rest of the world to let Him love them. Get caught up in doing what Jesus told us to do.

What will the results be? For me the results have been varied. I understood that Jesus wasn't just talking about telling with my mouth. He meant to tell the way that He told me, with Love, Joy, Peace, Patience, Kindness, Goodness, Gentleness, and Self-control. He wanted me to hold someone, listen, understand and give hope. He wanted me to ask and not demand, to look and not judge.

He taught me and He delivered me. He secured me inside Himself and set me free to be who I was always meant to be. He wanted me to believe in Him and His ways and to live it. He was counting on me to do only what He asked me to do. It was beautiful to know Him. It was life itself. He believed that I could tell others with my life and they would find Him. It didn't matter what I believed about my abilities or shortcomings. He picked me. He believes in me.

I started by telling my husband. Mike now has his own personal relationship with God. Same for our girls. We told our family, some checked out what we were telling them and had the same results, other family members think we are off the deep end and don't want us to tell them any more. (I pray that God sends someone else to tell them).

We told our friends about Jesus, some listened and asked questions. Some joined us in Bible studies and found Jesus for themselves. Some do not want to hang out with us any more because they think that God only deals with people when they die. And since they feel that most people try to be good, they believe that God has to let them into His presence when they do die.

I started telling everybody. I realized that just like I am praying for God to send someone to our family to reveal God's love, God is sending me to others families to do the same.

In a vision God taught me what it means when He sends us out. How God is one hundred percent positive we can accomplish what He is sending us to do. In this vision, I was sitting on a big floor playing with a lot of other kids. God the Father was watching out over all of us. The house was a big house and it was on a street like I have seen on the television in a place such as San Francisco where the hills are very steep. The house climbs up the hill, like a fortress following the road. Although the left and right sides of the street appear too be the same, the difference was that the house on the left was only one contin-uous house and not many built close together. The block went on for miles and the house on the left was tall, maybe five stories tall.

One of the neatest things I thought was the doors facing the street. Each door was a little different than the rest. Some had flashy colors painted on them and others looked weathered and a little worn. Some of the doors looked very inviting and others did not. Some were open and you could walk right in while others looked very heavy and hard to push open. But each door took you to the inside of the home of God the Father. It had many doors inside too. You could move from room to room and pass from what looked like building to building from the inside.

The interior back yard was huge, and was a safe place for everyone to go to play. There were many ways to come into the house all around the outside perimeter but you could only get to the safe cube like playground from the inside of the house. While in the playground it was very hard to think about all the people who were out walking on the street and did not come and live inside the House of God.

I was enjoying the meeting that was going on in one of the front rooms facing the outside street. Although I did not understand everything that was happening, or anything for that matter, I was welcome to sit and play with other children. That was until the noise from outside the house reached my ears stealing away my sense of peace.

Outside the house the enemy of the Lord was prowling around and yelling out bad things that he knew about people who were living in the house so that God the Father would hear. I could hear the things that he was saying, and although they were somewhat true, I didn't want him to tell my Father such bad things about me.

I looked up at God the Father; He was smiling at me so I continued to play. The enemy continued speaking louder about all the times I had sinned. I kept my ears on the sound coming from outside and my eyes on my Father.

My Father called me over to Him. He said "Laurie, I want you to take this money and go to the store and get me a gallon of milk." Now this was a familiar childhood memory. Many times in my life I was given money to go to the store and actually get a gallon of milk.

This upset me so much. I told my Father, "I can not go."

Then He smiled at me as I explained. "Father, the enemy is out there. He will try to steal this money, get me lost on the way to the store, try to convince me to buy something else when I get there, try to get me lost on the way home, he will try make me think that it is just too hard to do this task. Worst of all, he will try to make me think that You, Father, do not love me at all!"

My Father smiled at me and said, "Good, you know everything he will *try* to do!" But I understood that God, my Father, had given me a task that He knew I could achieve. He knew I had heard all the things that the enemy had said about me. He knew that I knew that He had heard it too. And even though this was being said, God still had chosen me. He allowed me to know the things that the enemy might *try*, but He also had absolute confidence in me, or He would never risk me leaving the safety of His presence. I understood that God wasn't sending me out because the enemy had taunted Him. The Father is not interested in what the enemy has to say. God was sending me out because He knew that I did not need to be afraid of the enemy and that I could do it. I can do it.

The Bible says that Jesus said, ***"All power in heaven and on earth is given to me. So go and make followers of all people in the world. Baptize them in the name of the Father and the Son and the Holy Spirit. Teach them to obey everything that I have taught you, and I will be with you always, even until the end of this age."*** **Matthew 28:18-20,** New Century Version

"Jesus said to his followers, 'Go everywhere in the world, and tell the Good News to everyone. Anyone who believes and is baptized will be saved, but anyone who does not believe will be punished. And those who believe will be able to do these things as proof: They will use my name to force out demons. They will speak in new languages. They will pick up snakes and drink poison without being hurt. They will touch the sick, and the sick will be healed." **Mark 16:15-18,** New Century Version.

I am positive God is still giving His children things to do. He has absolute confidence that we can do the task He had given us. I trust He believes I can go tell others about Him. So in April 2000, I began telling others about Him.

When I started telling people, more people started coming into our lives. Our lives started changing. Things started happening. Everything was changing and I mean it was changing fast. We were submerged in people and loving them through what they needed. We started feeding the college crowd and cooking for some of the elderly. What a difference acceptance makes. And more people came. It makes me so happy to know that loving people always works. We might not see the effect immediately, but it does change people and lives. The next thing we knew, we had people living with us. Not your normal everyday occurrence, but it started happening. It was sure something.

College people brought more college people. Everyone who entered our house was asked two questions. Are you hungry? And what local church do you attend? If you have ever lived in a college town, the answer to 'are you hungry' is 'yes'. So, over at least peanut butter and jelly sandwiches, we talked about Jesus and I checked to see if people had a personal relationship with Him. Many times we talked long into the night, and often times they returned to talk with Mike and I again and again. This is how we came to have so many children, and friends.

So get ready! God has big things He wants to do with you and me. He will encounter us in what ever way it takes for us to begin to know Him in ways that reveal His love.

I want to end with a prayer: "Jesus, thank you for loving me when I didn't love you back. Thank you for dying for me so that I can be free from sin. Thank you Jesus for choosing me and teaching me about who you are. Thank you for letting me be with you and giving me such an awesome thing to do. I want to 'Go tell others about you'. Thank you for helping me do it with my mouth and words, but always help me do it with my actions. Thank you Jesus, for making me feel like your favorite, would you help me to show others that you feel that way about them, too? I love You! In Jesus Name I pray. Amen